"Feeling confident as a parent is a rea
cover this joy. The eight principles in
sible. They provide keys to parenting
age. Kudos to Harris for this practical

—Michael Gurian,
author of *Nurture the Nature* and
The Wonder of Boys

"Bonnie Harris has written a truly informative, practical book that
will serve as an invaluable resource for parents and professionals
alike. She has skillfully described eight key principles that parents can follow as they raise their children to be more confident,
responsible, and resilient. Through real-life stories she offers realistic
examples of ways of practicing these principles and dealing with
situations that all parents face. She educates us with empathy, compassion, and humor. She is to be commended for writing such an
impressive book."
—Robert Brooks, Ph.D., Faculty, Harvard Medical School
Coauthor of *Raising Resilient Children* and
Raising a Self-Disciplined Child

"Revolutionary! Ms. Harris has done it again. What an eminently
practical book. She opens doors for a new way of thinking about
being a parent."
—Michael Trout, Director, The Infant-Parent Institute

"How I wish I had such a guide when I was a young parent! A
rich and very readable book loaded with accessible information and
analogies, carefully chosen examples, and thoughtfully constructed
solutions. The message that comes through loud and clear—Children are NOT problems, but rather they HAVE problems—should
be incorporated by both parents and professionals who work with
families."
—Elvin Kaplan, M.D.,
Assistant Professor of Pediatrics and
of Community and Family Medicine,
Dartmouth Hitchcock Medical Center

"In a sea of parenting books, this one stands out like a beacon. Her powerful insights rise above the noise, typical quick fixes and how-to tactics, and offer a rare two-way mirror for parents and children to truly see each other and connect. For life."

—Lu Hanessian, author of acclaimed memoir
Let the Baby Drive: Navigating the Road of New Motherhood
and host of *Make Room for Baby*,
Discovery Health Channel

■

"If you read just one parenting book this year, make it *Confident Parents, Remarkable Kids*. Bonnie's 8 Principles of Confident Parenting are easily applied to just about every situation, from mealtime struggles to bedtime arguments. Easy to read, with bulleted summaries and practical exercises at the end of each chapter, this book is sure to enhance, tweak, and improve every family's relationship. A must-read for parents who are looking for practical and empathic ways to deepen their connection with their children."

—Karen B. Walant, Ph.D., author of *Creating the Capacity for Attachment*, Board Member of Attachment Parenting International, and private practitioner

■

"Bonnie Harris sheds light on how to bridge the gap between negative behaviors and a positive parent/child relationship. *Confident Parents, Remarkable Kids* is a must-have parenting handbook on how to return to the essence of parenting: love, safety, understanding, and connection. The author offers a loving way to maintain boundaries while giving children unconditional love."

—Heather T. Forbes, LCSW
Beyond Consequences Institute

■

"Of the many ways Bonnie's eight principles support parenting through connection, my favorite is the way she changes our perception of challenging behavior from 'my child is being a problem' to 'my child is having a problem.'"

—Pam Leo, author of *Connection Parenting*

Confident
PARENTS
Remarkable
KIDS

Confident
PARENTS
Remarkable
KIDS

8 Principles for Raising Kids You'll *Love* to Live With

Bonnie Harris, M.S.Ed.,
bestselling author of *When Your Kids Push Your Buttons*

adamsmedia
Avon, Massachusetts

Copyright © 2008 by Bonnie Harris.
All rights reserved.
This book, or parts thereof, may not be reproduced in any
form without permission from the publisher; exceptions are
made for brief excerpts used in published reviews.

Published by
Adams Media, an F+W Publications Company
57 Littlefield Street, Avon, MA 02322. U.S.A.
www.adamsmedia.com

ISBN-10: 1-59869-471-5
ISBN-13: 978-1-59869-471-0

Printed in the United States of America.

J I H G F E D C B A

Library of Congress Cataloging-in-Publication Data
is available from the publisher.

This publication is designed to provide accurate and authoritative information
with regard to the subject matter covered. It is sold with the understanding
that the publisher is not engaged in rendering legal, accounting, or other
professional advice. If legal advice or other expert assistance is required, the
services of a competent professional person should be sought.

—From a *Declaration of Principles* jointly adopted by a Committee of the
American Bar Association and a Committee of Publishers and Associations

Many of the designations used by manufacturers and sellers to distinguish their
product are claimed as trademarks. Where those designations appear in this
book and Adams Media was aware of a trademark claim, the designations have
been printed with initial capital letters.

This book is available at quantity discounts for bulk purchases.
For information, please call 1-800-289-0963.

This book is dedicated to all parents
courageous enough to swim against the current.

ACKNOWLEDGMENTS

For the past twenty years, I have had the opportunity to work with parents around the globe and to help them understand their own and their children's behavior. I would not know how to do this without their stories, their desire to learn all they can about the most important job they will ever have, and their courage to change old patterns. For every parent I have worked with, I am eternally grateful.

A special thanks to my agent, Al Zuckerman, for his patience with my process in bringing this book to fruition and his belief in that process.

And to the many people who have helped and supported me in getting my work out to more and more parents. A few of them are: Kristin Frykman, Carol Lake, Liz Broderick, Carol Lunan, Lee Burwell, Deb Navas, Don McGillivray, Nancy Albanese, John and Melissa Hood, Beccy Goodhart, Amy Einhorn, Ping Wu, Jennifer Kushnier and Paula Munier at Adams Media, and my devoted and extremely patient husband, Baxter Harris. And my children, Molly and Casey, whom I have loved living with.

CONTENTS

INTRODUCTION

My children taught me two important lessons: Each child is completely different and requires different expectations, and neither punishment nor reward teaches anything worthwhile. By watching my children, discovering what helped and what didn't, I became fascinated with human behavior—why parents and children respond to each other the way they do and how that interaction affects children's future behavior and well-being.

When I read Louise Kaplan's *Oneness and Separateness: From Infant to Individual* in graduate school, I gained enormous empathy for the confusion and frustration of young children and learned the implications of misunderstanding their behavior. My son was only four at the time, but already I was sorry I hadn't had access to this information earlier. From then on, I devoted my parenting and my teaching to figuring out what children were going through and why they behaved the way they did. I learned to see life through the eyes of the child.

I brought up my children by the principles I write here—not as fully developed as what I teach now—and am pleased to report, first hand, on their effectiveness. My children are now adults and both embody the qualities I hoped they would have, as well as some I never anticipated. They are remarkable young people whom I admire tremendously. They learned to be respectful, responsible, caring people without punishment. They were a joy to live with—most of the time—and we continue to have a mutually loving relationship. If you don't want your children to leave the nest without so much as a glance backward, now is the time to begin focusing on and nurturing what you admire, respect, and love about them.

As a teacher of parent education over the past twenty years who has worked with parents in different parts of the world, I have learned a lot about what you want. You want to be the best parent you can be, but you get easily frustrated and say and do what you swore you wouldn't. You don't want to raise your children the way you were raised, but you're at a loss as to what to do instead. You want to teach your children right from wrong, but you know that the old ways don't work for your kids. Maybe you have learned that time-outs and punishment don't work, but when impatience or guilt gets the best of you, you fluctuate between empty threats and giving in. You are exhausted from daily power struggles and endless arguments and overwhelmed by the effort it takes in the limited time you have. You want your children to have the voice you never had, but when they use it, your button gets pushed, because they say and do what you never dared. You want desperately to do what is right, to have happy, responsible children, but your methods keep backfiring.

The world is different today; you are different. And your children have the advantage. They know you don't want to use force and fear tactics to raise them. They can speak their minds and be freer spirits. This is the good news. The bad news is that you may not know how to effectively set limits and say no without resorting to those fear tactics. And perhaps you are struggling with your own self-worth. You want your children to love you and are afraid of the reactions you will encounter if you say no. Or you say no but feel worn down when your children don't listen or do what you say. You want to be in control, but your children bring you to your knees. When parenting methods swing from best buddy to empty threats, your children find leverage. They learn that they will not be held accountable—not really. Hitting, yelling, grounding, and isolating don't work with most of today's kids because they won't stand for it. They are not afraid the way you were. They demand respect. But you misread their demands as acts of defiance and disrespect—because that's what your parents did.

The key to turning this around—to finding a better way—is a change in perception. Simple, but enormous. But you have to want to change and be committed to practice. It will seem like learning a foreign language. You might think you are letting your kids get away with something. It's hard at first to believe that fairness and logic can be effective discipline methods. Letting go of old habits is the hard part.

Your children need you to be in charge. That is your responsibility. But being in charge means keeping your cool and staying calm in the face of even the most difficult situations. It's easy to lose control; it's hard to stay detached enough to remain in charge. Each success story I hear from a parent includes, "I was able to stay calm" or "I didn't lose it."

We are not responsible for our children's feelings and behavior, but we are fully responsible for our own. Their behavior reflects what they experience. When we take responsibility for ourselves and stop trying to get our children to change, we change. When we act like the grownups we are meant to be, our children can act like the children they are—children you'll love to live with.

The eight principles presented in this book can change your life. They will help you develop your parenting philosophy. Having a core philosophy provides you with a reservoir from which to draw, so that whatever situation may arise or whatever your state of mind, your response is consistent and grounded. We need principles to rely on in times of stress, when we don't have time to think, when dinner is burning, when the baby is crying, when siblings are fighting, when we are impatient and tired, and when crisis hits. Holding these eight principles means that parenting decisions are consistent no matter what and yours and your children's needs are ensured and in balance. Add your personal and cultural values to these eight ingredients and your parenting will be a recipe for success.

You will always question and have doubts. You will make plenty of mistakes. You will never be perfect. But knowing you have dependable principles to rely on will inject your parenting with confidence. When doubting friends and relatives question your attitude and decisions, you will have solid ground to stand on. You will be able to explain your decisions, stand up to arguments, and even influence others toward more mindful parenting. Helping your children through their problems will bring you satisfaction and fulfillment. You will be amazed at how much easier it can be—and without reverting to those methods you hate. In fact, you can raise children who are a joy to live with and who will look to you for a safe and nurturing relationship throughout their lives.

Confident Parents, Remarkable Kids is the book you will wish your parents had read. The eight chapters in Part 1 fully describe each of the eight principles, illustrated with true stories throughout. The end of each chapter lists the main points and offers practices to help you apply the principles to your own life. Once you apply them, you will begin to look for and see your children's qualities and capabilities rather than irritations and inadequacies. You will understand their behavior as clues rather than calamities and learn to be a detective rather than a police officer. You will learn how to connect with your children, even in the toughest times, and teach them to problem-solve, take responsibility, and be accountable for their actions—without punishment or blame. And you will regain the authority that your children really do want you to have.

Part 2 takes you through seven aspects of a common, ordinary day in the life of seven families and shows you how the principles are applied. These stories are filled with suggestions for ways to solve daily dilemmas that can be adapted to your own family.

Although the stories in this book cover toddlers to preteens, the principles hold true throughout the entire course of your parent/child relationship.

Children are cooperative and respectful when there is balance in the family—like a mobile dancing in the breeze. But if one element of the mobile is too heavy, it will not dance. Equalize the weight, and balance is restored. When either your needs or your child's needs consistently hold more weight, the balance is off.

Learn the dance and find out how much more enjoyable life can be.

PART 1

THE EIGHT PRINCIPLES
OF CONFIDENT PARENTING

The First Principle:
My Child Wants to Be Successful

I hate you! You never let me have anything I want. I wish I had Jeff's mom. She lets him play that game all the time. You're so lame." Well practiced, eight-year-old Jared ran the familiar litany when Kathleen said no—again—to his plea for the video game that "everybody else gets to play." Telling Jared no to anything he wanted was a surefire invitation to meltdown. His begging was insatiable, the meltdowns frequent. No one could argue and wear Kathleen down like Jared, her most stubborn child—number three out of her four children. She knew the arguing and hurtful remarks wouldn't stop until he was asleep that night and she fell exhausted and disheartened into bed. Successful was the last word Kathleen would use to describe Jared's behavior.

"Every day it's something else," she complained. "Can I have that? I have to do this…. He drives me crazy! I swear I just don't like him sometimes. He makes me yell until I'm hoarse, then he laughs at me! I send him to his room, put him in time-out, take away privileges…. I've tried everything and nothing works. Why can't he just do what I ask—ever? Why does life have to be like this?"

Life doesn't have to be like this. The problem for Kathleen is that the "everything" she has tried is a series of techniques that keep her spinning in a vicious cycle, leading her into a sequence of fears and expectations that set children like Jared up for failure again and again. He doesn't stand a chance.

Kathleen is a loving and caring mother. Her intentions are good, but her frustrations overwhelmed her. She regularly assumed that Jared was going to be a pain in the neck before he even opened his mouth. She knew she would spend her day simply trying to get through it without a meltdown. She believed that the only way to get him in line was with control, but mostly she felt out of control. Punishments didn't work. He resisted her threats and just got angrier. She blamed him. She blamed herself. When blame and control set the foundation of a relationship, nothing works. And nothing did until Kathleen found a way to step outside her box—her familiar frame of perceptions and expectations—to see Jared differently and to respond to him instead of react. After that, the whole family dynamic began to change.

At the end of her rope, Kathleen came to me for counseling. It was soon clear that her perception of Jared kept her stuck in frustration and anger. Her focus was on his failures. So Jared saw himself reflected in her eyes as a failure. Kathleen needed to step into Jared's shoes to see what his world looked like to him, to hear what her words sounded like, and to change what her eyes, voice, and body language were communicating to him. She couldn't change him, but she could change how she saw him.

We revisited scene after scene in which his stubbornness, arguing, and cutting remarks revealed at a deeper level his need to be heard. But since Kathleen took his behavior at face value and saw him only as defiant and rude, he had to push harder and louder in his attempt to make her listen. He didn't know how to say, "Hey Mom, all you need to do is accept me. I get all wound up when I think that you hate me and wish I were more like my brother." All Jared could do was try to reach her with his behavior—his cue that he felt frustrated, confused, and misunderstood. He was reacting to expectations that told him he could never get it right. He'd come to believe he was a pain, and so he acted that way. Kathleen didn't understand his cues or her own expectations. It never occurred to her that she and her husband were the ones who needed to change first.

Basic Trust

Children want to be successful. No child is happy being manipulative or out of control. Success, in this context, is defined as a sense of personal rightness and accomplishment in one's developing ability to express needs and have them met, of being in balance or alignment with oneself and one's world, to be in a state of regulation or stability. A successful child feels confident in himself and emotionally secure. His behavior is appropriate to his temperament and stage of development. This definition of success has nothing to do with the acquisition of things, money, or accomplishments but with inner balance and well-being.

At the core of raising a successful child must be a basic trust in the individual and the developmental process.

It requires parents to step back and watch; to understand and trust the child's motives and to learn who he is and what he is capable of before stepping in to censor his behavior.

As soon as Kathleen got it, guilt flooded her. Now she worried that she had damaged Jared for life. I convinced her that to change her perception would feel like a gift to him—once he trusted that her change was genuine. Such healing can happen at any time. Sometimes it's immediate and sometimes it takes time, but it is never too late. With practice and continued awareness of her reactions, Kathleen was able to see that different perceptions of Jared's behavior helped him. Trusting these new perceptions was the hard part. But soon she could see that he really was trying hard. He wasn't out to get her or wear her down. It was her fears telling her that. So she decided to give him a chance.

"Oh, man, look at this!" Jared exclaimed as he and his mother approached a display of CD players on their way to the toy department to fetch a birthday present for Jared's friend. "Okay, here it comes," Kathleen thought. "Can I do it?" She instantly played out the old battle they would have had in her head. Jared had broken his CD player, he would beg for a new one. In the old script she would say something like, "No, Jared! Come on, hurry up. I told you we weren't getting anything but the birthday present. I have a thousand things to do today, and I don't have time for this. If you hadn't been so clumsy with yours..." Blah, blah, blah. It was always the same, she now realized. Nothing horrible, nothing abusive, but now she could see how her old reactions had that critical tone that set him up to be defensive, stubborn, and a pain in the neck.

This time she thought of a different script and decided to take the time. She stopped and looked at what drew his attention. "Yeah, they're pretty cool. All different colors. And all different prices. What are the features that make some more expensive than others?"

Jared looked up at his mother in shock.

"Is it the different headphones?" Kathleen added gamely.

After Jared became convinced this was indeed his mother, he was delighted and proud to educate her on the players' features. Kathleen was amazed at his knowledge. She noticed his whole body relax. He had been anticipating a fight that didn't happen.

"So if you were to buy one, do you think a more expensive one would be worth the money?"

Again, he enthusiastically explained which he would pick and why. Then came the inevitable—"So can I get one?"

Without a pause, Kathleen said calmly, "I'm not going to buy you one. But can you think of a way to get one yourself?" After a moment of disappointment, the boy's wheels started spinning. Jared then came up with a plan to clean the garage and rake leaves. Now his impatience switched from getting his Mom to give in to him to buying the birthday present fast so he could get home and start earning money. It took some time and reminding, but Jared did eventually earn the money. "The look on his face when he paid for the CD player was worth the wait," Kathleen reported with pride. "I never would have thought this could happen."

Intention for Success

Instead of pushing ahead with her own agenda, expecting Jared to follow suit—something that never failed to provoke him—Kathleen stopped to see his agenda. He hadn't meant to be manipulative or stubborn. He was merely looking after his own interest, wanting to share it with his mother, and hoping to get what he wanted—frustrating, yes, but normal and completely understandable.

When a parent sees a child's will as manipulative, disobedient, and stubborn, fears take over and reactions abound. The child's integrity must fend off these angry reactions. The fending off is usually perceived as misbehavior. But the misbehavior is the child's attempt to be successful and in balance. When a child like Jared fends off, his behavior is usually loud, disagreeable, inconvenient, and disruptive—hardly behavior a parent sees as an attempt at being successful.

Jared is an impulsive, distractible, and energetic boy who has a harder time than his siblings cooperating with his mother's agenda and sticking with it. Having a better understanding of his temperament now, Kathleen sees the disconnect she had created because of anticipating his nagging, begging, and arguing. Her expectation of Jared evoked his resistance and the behavior she feared. Now that she can understand his point of view, she is calmer and can set more effective limits on his behavior—preventing some and letting go of some.

Kathleen's husband came on board after he saw the changes. Now they rarely assume Jared is up to no good or will never listen. They see his struggle first. They acknowledge that the circumstances at the time—the clash of agendas, their expectations of him, the level of stress he is feeling—can create his resistance. It's not that he refuses to cooperate—it's that right then, he can't. All they focused on before was getting him to change. All they knew was to criticize and punish. But once they understood that Jared wanted to be successful, even when his behavior looked otherwise, Jared began to see himself as more successful in their eyes.

Jared did not morph into an easygoing child. His temperament still presents many difficulties. But now his parents' expectations of him are based on who he is, not on who they wish he would be. Their acceptance of him goes a long way toward gaining his cooperation.

Walking Off the Battlefield

Children feel under attack from negative judgments and criticisms and are often left with no choice but to engage in counterattack. If the perceived enemy remains invested in hostility (power struggle), it is the rare child who can back off and change his behavior. Most adults and certainly children think that withdrawing from the attack leaves them too vulnerable. So they persist in a fight to the finish. Defensive reactions appear to be the only chance of surviving the onslaught of criticisms and blame.

We do a good job teaching our children strategic maneuvers to get what they want in the power struggles we engage in. But if the parent behaves like a grownup, she will be the first to leave the battlefield.

This doesn't mean that Kathleen always has to do it Jared's way. But if she had been unable to stop to look at the CD players, she could have respectfully said, "Wow, those CD players do look great, don't they? I'm really sorry we can't stop this time. I have so much to do, and I have to ask you to keep going. I appreciate you doing this for me." Jared would have been frustrated, he might even have had a meltdown. But he also would have felt accepted, which has a cumulative effect just as the opposite does. If Kathleen wants him to respect her, it must start with her respect of him. When she is able to see it his way, he will be more able to do it her way when he has to.

When a child perceives that his parent thinks he is bad, he believes he is bad, so he behaves badly. His defenses go up, and he is tense with readiness for the daily power struggles that he must try to win. Better behavior is unlikely until he gets a different message from his parent.

Children Are More Capable Than We Think

Understanding that children want to be successful implies a trust in the child's capability, which is fostered by encouragement and correction, never by disapproval. Sometimes that support means stepping in to help the child get back on track by setting limits or problem solving, and sometimes it means trusting the child's own process.

A mother relayed to me her story of moving from the East to the Midwest with two young children, four and two and a half. Just before they moved, the mother broke her foot and was in a cast for weeks. She was on crutches for a few of those weeks and quite immobile for the rest. Through the move and unpacking in the new house, her children stepped up to the plate and demonstrated cooperation, helpfulness, and empathy for their mother. When we either don't—or in this case, can't—do everything we think we should for our children, they have the chance to show us how capable they are.

7

I recall watching my daughter soon after she had mastered walking. She was climbing the steps on her toy slide and sliding down—over and over again. She was so intent on her work that she forgot I was in the room. I didn't remind her. Often she would climb to the top and fall or trip on a step. Each time, she got up and tried it again—always differently—until she got it. I watched in awe at her determination and learned how capable she was of correcting her mistakes. I continued watching throughout her childhood and found again and again that trusting her, although not always easy, paid off. Even though many of the decisions she has made in her twenty-something years have been frustrating, worrisome, or not ones I would have made, I have learned that by walking away from battles I could have so easily engaged in, her decisions have turned out to be right for her. With basic trust in capability comes acceptance—a need more powerful even than love—even in the face of misbehavior.

Born for Success

Human beings are programmed for success. We are born with the instincts to cue our environment correctly to get our basic needs met. Babies suck to get food; they cry to be comforted or fed. Nourishment and attachment are basic needs. Withholding food or comfort ("You're teaching her that crying will get her what she wants.") is punishment intended to stop the crying. When her cues are not answered, she does not learn to stop crying, she learns to distrust her cues. Then she has to try harder. So she cries louder—until that doesn't work either.

By training children with our methods to get the behavior we want, we can unintentionally teach our children to distrust their own instincts.

When a child's cues are answered, she learns that she is capable—that she is successful.

Just as instinctive as the urge to cry and suck is the urge to belong. Humans are social animals. We have lived in society since the beginning of time. We instinctively know how to get along. But we routinely parent with the assumption that our children cannot get along until we socialize them. If a two-year-old doesn't share his toys, his parent fears selfishness and then attempts to train him to share at an age before his impulses can accommodate sharing. His parent does not trust that socialization will come in due time and interrupts his natural course with attempts at teaching proper behavior.

With a belief that children want to be successful, we watch the child's development unfold and trust her developmental process. We expect that she is a unique individual and may socialize differently than others—she may be more shy or more outgoing, introverted or extroverted. But we will help her find her way of appropriate socializing. We distract the two-year-old from pulling a toy away from another child, understanding that she is not yet ready to share. When she is a little older and no longer distractible, we teach her to take turns by calmly helping her do it, assuring her she will get her turn soon. We make sure that happens. If she screams in dismay, we comfort her, acknowledging her frustration and reassuring her she will get her toy back. We do not take the toy back and give it to her, nor do we take the toy away to teach her a lesson. With steady practice, without yelling, criticizing, or punishing, she slowly learns that she can let go and the toy will return. We have confidence in her natural ability to learn when she is ready and patience to stay the course until she is. We trust that she wants to do it right.

If we yell at her or put her in time-out for grabbing the toy, she learns that she is bad for wanting it. She is confused. So she starts to build her defense, which is her natural instinct to protect herself from attack. Then whenever someone has something she wants, she fights harder and sneakier to get it. We perceive her as mean and manipulative. But she's not being manipulative on purpose, she has learned what she has to do to get what she wants.

Getting Off Track and into the Vicious Cycle

Our traditional reward and punishment method of parenting implies that a child is naturally unruly and disobedient and requires training to be otherwise. So we train the child to listen, not to his internal cues, but to his parents, who always know best.

Like it or not, we set our children up to grow dependent on someone else to tell them whether or not they are okay.

Natural connection to internal cues is broken, internal balance is off, and the child is thrown off track and misbehaves. The parent reacts punitively to the misbehavior, and families become entrenched in the vicious cycle.

Punishments and rewards train the child to behave the way the parent wants and society expects. We disregard what the child needs—usually out of ignorance, not malice—and try to get the child to do what we want "for his own good."

Tired parents get to the end of their rope quickly, yell, grab, slap, and manipulate to get their children to stop crying, stop demanding, just stop. These angry, critical reactions are met with resistance from children who are not getting their basic needs of respect and acceptance met. Resistant behaviors further provoke angry reactions from parents who don't understand the emotional roots of the behavior. Their reactions incite further misbehavior and the cycle spins, often out of control.

Many parents don't know how to step off the cycle. They expect their child to. They assume children will self-correct with punishments or negative reactions. But that's not how cycles work. The irony is that, except for the temperamentally adaptable who obey easily, strong-willed children resist controls and inconvenience life for their parents, prompting further controls and reprimands.

The Autocratic Expectation

"But there's got to be a line. I have to put my foot down. After all, I'm the parent, and he has to do what I say." Certainly authority is important. But when punishment is used to control behavior, the child behaves out of fear. Fear creates stress. Stress causes the child to either submit or react depending on her temperament. The child who is punished doesn't sit pensively contemplating what she just did and how to do it better next time. She is usually angry, resentful, or revengeful. She then defends herself against what she thinks will get her in trouble next time by lying, cheating, laughing, ignoring, hiding, sneaking, running away.

And yes, yelling may get her to stop—this time. Punishment often works at getting a desired result—today. But at what cost? What is the long-term learning? Quick-fix solutions that use fear to motivate offer short-term results. This mindset rules out a thought such as, *She is trying to be successful but something is pulling her off track.* By holding all the power, autocratic parents undermine the child's growing capability, initiative, and basic instinct to succeed.

THE BOX

Put a plant in a sunny window, water it regularly, keep it healthy, and it will grow and blossom. Now put a box over the plant with a hole on one side. The plant will bend toward the hole, toward the sunlight. It will probably stay alive, but it will never be lush and healthy and will likely never blossom. The child is like this plant. The box represents the oppression of punishment. When punished, even when abused, the child is capable of bending toward the light attempting to reach approval and acceptance. But the box creates an obstacle that pulls him off track, requiring him to shift off his center and relinquish a strong sense of self. He too may never blossom.

The Permissive Expectation

Many parents too easily relinquish authority due to lack of confidence, too much stress, too little time, or fear of emotions. They may believe that it is healthy for children to express themselves—an experience they may never have had. They may dread their child's anger and confront or deny as little as possible. These children rarely experience disappointment and are slow in developing coping skills. They are often left without the structure they require to learn self-discipline, delayed gratification, respect, and empathy.

Often parents believe they must continually reaffirm how special their children are to build self-esteem. So permissive parents defer power to the child. Now the balance is off in the other direction. Children take the reins when no one else will—not because they want to but because they can. Either compensating for the parent's autocratic upbringing, assuaging the guilt of a working parent, or avoiding the child's unhappiness, the overly permissive parent is willing to give and give to meet the child's every desire.

But when the child does not appreciate the parent's sacrifice ("after all I've done, and she won't even put her clothes away"), resentment sets in ("How dare you behave that way?"). The parent may quickly swing to his automatic, knee-jerk reaction—the autocratic parenting he experienced—and blow. Then guilt or hopelessness takes over, and the parent defers to the child even more. A different kind of cycle spins. Both autocratic and permissive parenting creates obstacles for the child's innate drive toward success.

Any child takes what is given, comes to expect whatever treatment is received, and behaves accordingly.

If she is thwarted at every turn, she will redirect by learning devious strategies, modeled by her parents, to get what she wants. If she is always allowed what she wants, she will expect it every time. This is not the child's initial intention but what she has learned to expect. Neither suppressed nor entitled children respect or have empathy for others. They shirk responsibility and lay blame for their actions elsewhere.

Seven-and-a-half-year-old Maribeth wore her mother, Anne, down with demands. She wanted to go skiing, but after Anne packed her and her two siblings in the car and arrived at the ski slope, Maribeth claimed that her mother had brought the wrong poles—"These aren't mine. What did you bring the wrong ones for?" She refused to ski and wanted to go home. Nothing could appease her—"I'm not going to ski, and you can't make me!"—until her mother took them all home. The following week when the day for the ski program rolled around again, her mother asked Maribeth rather sarcastically, "So what is it, are we going to go skiing tomorrow or not?" Maribeth said yes, but on the drive up, she complained that it was too cold, blamed her mother for bringing the wrong jacket, and again refused to ski and insisted on going home.

Maribeth is not a born spoiled brat. She has been given the freedom to decide whether they stay or go—a decision that gives her too much power. As with most young children, Maribeth's mind changes rapidly, and she hasn't learned that everyone's needs are as important as her own. Anne's desire to make her daughter happy has set Maribeth up to take advantage of that desire.

With a belief that her child wants to be successful, Anne can ask herself what is blocking Maribeth from behaving appropriately. When she can look for the obstacle, perhaps she can see that too much choice is giving her too much power. Once Maribeth decides she would like to take part in the ski program with her brothers, her choices narrow. "Tomorrow is the ski program. Make sure you have your equipment and the clothes you want to wear together and ready." If Maribeth decides she doesn't want to ski, or has forgotten her poles, she can choose between staying in the child-care program, with a friend in the lodge (if available), or go skiing anyway—true consequences. Going home is not an option as it is not considerate of three other people. These expectations recognize that Maribeth is capable of taking responsibility for her own gear as well as handling disappointment if she makes a mistake.

Children learn best when there is a structure of limits and appropriate expectations they can count on and when they know their parents are in charge. Discipline is needed, but discipline that builds responsibility and conscience.

Mirrors Cast Spells

Our eyes see our children at their best and their worst. Our eyes are their mirrors. If we want to insure self-confidence and security, our eyes must reflect our children as successful (unconditional love), even when they are at their worst.

It is often not as important what we say or do, but how we do it—our tone, attitude, and body language speak volumes and cast "spells" on our children. We are responsible for whether that spell is a good spell or a bad one.

14

Maribeth is struggling under a bad spell. Jared is coming out from under one. What kind of a spell were you brought up under? Are you still under it?

Our feeling state sends strong messages, both positive and negative, to our children. To behave appropriately, children need a consistent message, a positive spell that says, *I trust that you want to do what is right.* When this is the spell despite inevitable tantrums, out-of-control impulsivity, disobedience, and natural, egocentric behavior, that child becomes the child you will love to live with, the child who is fun to be around.

As we perceive, so we experience. As the Nobel Prize–winning physicist, Max Planck, said, "When you change the way you look at things, the things you look at change." When your child has become an inert blob on the couch in front of the television or computer, your perception of him as a slug accompanied by the assumption that he's a lazy bum and the fear that he will never accomplish anything in life, much less do his homework, will perpetuate his sluglike behavior. Reprimands and criticisms support the expectation of a slug. The picture of a slug is what he sees in your eyes, so he will continue sluglike behavior. He is under the slug spell.

To affect this behavior, temporarily put the behavior aside and look to the nature of the child and this first principle. This is difficult when the frame you have been using tells you that taking away TV privileges will teach him to get his act together. The least likely outcome is that punishment will motivate your child. The most likely is that he will be angry and defiant, and you will be inconsistent with the punishment. When you accept that your child wants to be successful, you will see that he doesn't particularly like the life of a slug either, but he doesn't know what else to do right now. You will look for a way to help rather than criticize. You understand that he is temporarily out of balance with himself. You might engage him in activities with you or create opportunities for him. You can set limits on television viewing, and he can hear you—he doesn't have to like it—if you are accepting, not punishing. It's all in the way you see him.

Remember, the obstacle that is in your child's way of behaving successfully is an opportunity—your child's opportunity to grow beyond and learn from that obstacle, and your opportunity to help your child overcome it and feel fulfillment in the connection.

Main Ideas from Chapter 1:

- A successful child feels inner balance and well-being.
- No child wants to be manipulative or out of control.
- Misbehavior indicates an obstacle in the way of the child's success.
- A child is born with natural capabilities and instincts toward socialization.
- Punishments and rewards can pull a child off his natural course and undermine his innate drive toward success.
- Walking away from battles can instill trust in the child's capabilities.
- Children cannot be expected to be the first to step off the vicious cycle.
- Natural consecutive stages of development are often interfered with by coercive, punitive training methods of untrusting, impatient parents.
- Rewards and punishments are intended to make parents' lives easier. They do not help the child get back on track where successful behavior is common.
- Punishment creates fear. Fear equals stress. Stress leads to misbehavior.
- Good discipline builds responsibility and conscience. Poor discipline, either autocratic or permissive, creates suppressed or entitled children who lay blame elsewhere for their actions.

- A parent's words, tone of voice, and body language have the power to cast both positive and negative spells over children that can last a lifetime.

Practice:

1. The next time you feel frustrated with your child, become aware of where your mind is taking you, what your perception is telling you. Are you expecting misbehavior? Are you fostering your child's abilities and independence or incompetence and dependence by your reactions?
2. Consciously switch to thinking, *If he wants to be successful, what is it that is in his way? Is it emotions, feeling blamed, certain people, an event that has occurred? What is causing the stress?*
3. Notice how your feelings change when you think this way.
4. Realize that he is probably unable to deal with whatever the obstacle is and ask yourself, *How can I help?* Example: *She gets really frustrated and angry when her brother is around and fights with him a lot. If it is to get my attention, what can I do? I can pay attention to the times when she is especially aggressive, see if there is a pattern, and anticipate it by giving her a little one-on-one time.*

CHAPTER 2

The Second Principle: Behavior Is My Clue

When my daughter, Molly, was four, I had a pivotal lesson in punishment. For whatever reason I can no longer remember, I sent her to her room. She stomped up the stairs and slammed the door. That was fine. I didn't expect her to be happy about it. Fortunately I remained in the kitchen near the large picture window. Out of the corner of my eye, I saw movement and looked just in time to see Molly running off. She had climbed out her window onto the roof of the porch, shimmied down the post, and took off. I finally found her hiding under a large bush beyond the barn.

Many parents would have punished her for running off, but I took her behavior to mean that if I punished her, she would feel wronged and would pay me back—as hard as she could. That's who she was. I decided right then and there that a retaliatory relationship was not what I wanted to have with her. I had to find a better way. She has never been punished since. It took me four years to learn the lesson, but when I looked at her behavior as my clue to what she needed instead of an indictment, our relationship changed. I've never regretted letting go of punishment.

The Meaning of Behavior

Your child's behavior is your indicator of his well-being. The behavior is your clue, your signal to the internal emotional state that lies beneath the behavior and triggers it—even the awful, annoying, embarrassing, exhausting behavior. It's what tells you how your child is doing. Be grateful for it. It's all you have to let you know what your child needs. What she doesn't have is words and an understanding of what is going on—it's all there in her behavior. You just have to put your detective hat on to uncover the cause.

Adults are quite capable of keeping their internal emotions under wraps, but children are raw—thank goodness. They don't know yet how to keep a lid on it. What specifically is generating the behavior may not be apparent. It's not always necessary to know.

> *What is necessary—what makes all the difference*
> *in how we handle the behavior—is the perception*
> *that the behavior you see is rooted in something*
> *real—a deeper emotional state.*

If the behavior is developmentally and temperamentally appropriate, you can rest assured your child is doing fine. When at age three or four she has climbed onto the counter to get the flour she has seen you use and makes a cake with it all over the kitchen floor, her behavior is plenty annoying but age appropriate. She is doing fine. If your morning dawdler holds back, resists getting dressed, and is hard to remove from television, his temperament may be telling you that he is a slow mover and has a difficult time with transitions. He is also fine. But if the behavior is inappropriate, out of control, and unusual to your child's temperament and stage of development, then it is telling you that your child is out of balance, in turmoil, and has a need that is not being met—your child is not a happy camper. So when that resistant, defiant behavior shows up, and you understand that this behavior is your clue that your child is hurting, and you know that he wants to be successful, your perception will automatically change from *my child is being a problem to my child is having a problem.* You will understand that there is an obstacle in your child's way of success.

Taking Behavior at Face Value

Typically we look at behavior at face value only. Our primary concern is that the child does what we want. If she is too noisy, a bother, asks too many questions, and whines and tantrums to get what she wants, we tell her, "Be quiet, don't bother me, and stop whining." Depending on the degree of our annoyance, we may coerce, threaten, yell, hit, reprimand, or isolate her to get what *we* want. She will feel misunderstood, angry, accused, bad, and will have no recourse but to take whatever punishment is doled out. Depending on her temperament, she will either act out these feelings with more misbehavior, repress her feelings and learn she is wrong to have them, or seek revenge by tormenting a sibling, friend, or pet—thereby signaling her problem again.

Webster defines behavior as the aggregate of responses to internal stimuli and external stimuli. In other words, behavior is the expression of how a child feels on the inside when faced with what is coming at him from the outside. Whether it be a parent, sibling, teacher, friend, or event, that external condition reacts with internal emotions and results in behavior. The behavior can tell us what is going on if we pay attention. We must be a detective and use the clues of the behavior to get to the need.

To affect our child's behavior, his internal state must first be understood, then accepted, then addressed.

Looking for the Roots

Think of behavior metaphorically. Your child's misbehavior is like weeds in a garden. If you don't like the way the weeds look you can yank them away so they can't be seen. But as any gardener knows, a quick removal means reappearance in a day or two. If you take the time to get down and dirty and dig out the roots, the weeds will be gone.

Punishing behavior is like grabbing at the weeds. It is a temporary fix. But by digging to the roots of the behavior, addressing the emotional state and underlying need, the behavior itself will disappear.

The expressing behavior may result from a present situation (a tantrum over being told no), or it can represent a cumulative effect that seems a mystery ("Where did that come from? All I said was, 'It's time to get your coat on,' and he acted like I'd told him to jump out the window."). Cumulative effects build up and root deeply, often requiring additional, outside detective work from a professional. If the balance of power is off, for example, and the child feels powerless too often (the autocratic model), that growing sense of powerlessness can erupt over being told to put a coat on. You may think he is unreasonable or overly sensitive. Possibly you yell or punish. A power struggle ensues. To address the internal cause requires more than just forgetting about the coat. It needs an evaluation of power in the family.

Question what the person or circumstance (external stimuli) is asking or expecting of the child. Is the external condition adding too much pressure, setting unrealistic expectations, presenting too much stimulation, or being disrespectful?

Lauren had been attempting to get her very outspoken and determined three-and-a half-year-old, Caroline, away from her play date and home so she could have dinner ready on time for once. The evening, bedtime, and Caroline's behavior the next day depended on an early, smooth dinnertime. Lauren had exhausted all her tricks, such as five-minute, three-minute, and one-minute warnings and, "Tucker will be so hungry if you don't get home to feed him." Embarrassed in front of the friend's mother, Lauren thought her daughter was rude and disobedient, so she pulled out the empty-threat trick she hated. "If you don't come right now, you won't be able to come back here again." She knew she wouldn't carry through with it, but it worked, so she kept using it.

Caroline started to climb in the car when she saw her Barbie doll lying on the backseat. She shrieked gleefully, "Oh I forgot, I have to show Annie my Barbie!" grabbed the doll, and started to run back. Lauren grabbed Caroline's arm and shouted right in her face, "No you will not. You have taken way too long to leave and now you are coming with me." Caroline hit her mother on the arm with her Barbie doll. Lauren grabbed Barbie out of Caroline's hand, yelled at her, and shoved her into her car seat. Fuming, Lauren drove with a tightly clenched jaw listening to Caroline's screaming all the way home. The rest of the evening was a nightmare as Caroline refused to eat, angrily resisted everything Lauren asked her to do, and didn't get to sleep until 9:30. Exhausted, angry, and feeling like a failure, Lauren fell into bed dreading the next morning.

This kind of situation is not fair to either Lauren or Caroline. Look at what the behaviors are signaling regarding Caroline's internal state. Caroline didn't want to stop having fun at her friend's house (age-appropriate internal stress over having to leave), and when she was confronted by the threat of not coming again (external condition), she felt trapped (increased internal stress). Finding her Barbie brought excitement again, but her angry mother grabbed her arm (external condition suddenly increasing the stress), and she reacted impulsively (age-appropriate release of tension) by hitting her mother (her expressed behavior). She was immediately yelled at and forced into the car. Her only option was to defend herself, and at three, she had few coping skills to do much more than scream to release her tension (expressed behavior).

Her need was to be accepted for her desires and to have her agenda (showing the Barbie doll) at least acknowledged if not allowed.

But Lauren was feeling her own frustration and was too focused on her agenda of getting home to be able to acknowledge Caroline's. Lauren expected Caroline to climb aboard her agenda and relinquish her own.

Parent as Detective

By viewing Caroline's behavior as a clue that has roots to something deeper, let's see how things could be different. If Lauren were detecting roots, even with little patience left, she would see that Caroline was frustrated and upset rather than rude and disobedient, allowing Lauren to have a bit more compassion. Understanding Caroline's persistent temperament and developmental lack of impulse control, Lauren could put the clues together to come up with a better way to manage her daughter's behavior.

First, Lauren and Caroline need a plan for leaving a play date. They can work it out ahead of time, so when it comes time to leave and Caroline doesn't remember the plan, Lauren can calmly say, "Let's follow our agreement. Do you want to walk yourself or shall I carry you to the car?" If Lauren knows that Caroline wants to be successful, she will understand that something is in her way of cooperating, in this case her impulsivity (stage of development) and persistence (temperament), not disobedience or manipulation. Caroline's behavior would still be frustrating but would not feel so much like an attack.

When Caroline resists leaving (persistent temperament), Lauren would say, "Of course you don't want to go. You're having so much fun (giving her validation). What is the first thing you will tell Tucker about when we get home?" If this doesn't motivate Caroline, Lauren would give her the choice of going herself or being carried to the car—even if it causes tears.

When Caroline sees Barbie in the backseat, Lauren could either decide this is a battle not worth fighting, thereby relinquishing a few minutes rather than the whole evening, or acknowledge Caroline's agenda and balance it with her own. "Oh Caroline, I wish I could take the time to let you run back with Barbie. I just don't have any more time today." As Caroline cries, Lauren can give her a hug and acknowledge how much she wants to show Barbie and how sad she must feel. "I bet Barbie would like to meet your friend too. Let's make sure that next time we come Barbie comes too. What would you like her to wear when she comes?"

There is no guarantee of a cheerful ride home, but it is likely that Caroline's internal state will be more sad than angry so the screaming may be less intense, would eventually subside, and the rest of the evening could go smoothly. The problem came for Caroline when her mother did not acknowledge her agenda but expected her to go along with what her mother wanted.

When our children are acting out,
they are trying to tell us something.

If Caroline had the words and the maturity, she could have told her mother that she wasn't intending to make her late, nor was she intending to be inconsiderate or disobedient when she saw her doll and wanted to show it to her friend. She was just wanting to stay. When she hit her mother with the doll, her behavior meant, "Hey, you're treating me like I'm a bad kid. You're yelling at me and grabbing me, and I don't like it. I'm mad at you."

Even then, if Lauren could have detached enough after expressing her anger about being hit to see the behavior as a clue (the weeds), she could have prevented the rest of the day from going downhill by acknowledging Caroline's anger (one of the roots). "You must be really mad at me to hit me like that. You're mad because I won't let you take Barbie back in (addressing the internal state). I can understand that. You may not hit me, but you can tell me how mad you are." Caroline's anger must be allowed so she does not learn that she is wrong for feeling angry. It's the hit that is not okay. If the root of the hit is addressed, then the hit needn't happen again.

If Lauren is not able to detach, she can play detective after her emotions calm and come back to the situation later to address Caroline's internal state. "Remember when we both had a very bad time leaving Annie's house? I didn't like how either of us behaved, and I'd like to do a do-over." Lauren can acknowledge Caroline's frustration and anger, as well as her own at not being able to leave when she wanted and then being hit. When emotions are calm and the situation is behind them, Caroline is more likely to spontaneously apologize (demanding an apology never works) for hitting her mother, thereby making amends that will help her internal state of balance. They can talk about how they would each handle the situation differently, making a plan for next time; problem solving made simple. Lauren would have the opportunity to model owning up to a mistake, apologizing, and holding Caroline accountable for her part.

Understanding Misbehavior: Seeing the Obstacle

If we accept the principle that children want to be successful, then it holds true that children don't intend misbehavior.

In other words, children never misbehave for the sake of misbehaving but only as an expression of stress. In their book, *Beyond Consequences, Logic, and Control*, Heather T. Forbes and B. Bryan Post say, "All negative behavior arises from an unconscious, fear-based state of stress." In this light, misbehavior is viewed as a sudden impulse or mistake, not as an attack, intentional manipulation, or failure. When behavior becomes manipulative, it is through learning its power of grabbing attention, albeit negative.

*When misbehavior is continually misunderstood, a pattern
of failure sets in, and the out-of-balance, unsuccessful child
spends a good deal of time in fight or defense mode.*

His fragile sense of self tries to fight off what doesn't feel right when his basic needs are not being met. He doesn't understand it, so he acts out with behavior to signal his parents that he needs help. Understood this way, punishing misbehavior adds insult to injury and makes no sense.

With the understanding that my child wants to be successful, misbehavior is viewed as a defensive reaction to meeting an obstacle. In other words, when I see misbehavior, I will think, *My child is having a problem because something is blocking him from being successful.* My perception has switched 180° from my previous one that he is doing it on purpose, that he is being a problem. My emotion changes from anger to compassion. I know he wants to be successful on the other side of the obstacle. So I can be more objective, less reactive, in handling the behavior.

The reward and punishment system actually sets up misbehavior by creating obstacles. Its fundamental premise holds that children are basically unruly and uncooperative unless trained to behave properly. Rewards and punishments act counter to trust. Coercive methods are believed necessary to keep the unruly from getting out of control. Parents believe they are teaching responsibility, but they are demanding obedience to an external authority. The punitive system demands that children do as parents say no matter what. When children resist those demands and turn parent-deaf, parents feel distraught and often lash out in anger—increasing the child's obstacles. The result is parents who feel like failures and children who resist authority, ignore their own instincts, and do not know how to develop the internal controls that promote responsible behavior.

Hearing Instead of Reacting

Let's say that an eleven-year-old named Lisa, in a sudden outburst, has just screamed at her father, "You just don't get it do you? You are so lame. What century do you live in, anyway?" He perhaps said something innocuous like, "You're not wearing that are you?" If her father decides to send her to her room for her rude, disrespectful behavior, he is pulling at the weeds and missing the roots of her behavior. Lisa will likely be left fuming. She will feel resentful and misunderstood, and her anger will continue to build, waiting for it's next release. Connection between the two of them has been ruptured, and communication will be very difficult. The cause of her outburst, the root of her behavior, is unattended, and her father will likely assume that she is being a bratty preadolescent who must be taught her place. The seeds of future teenage rebellion are planted.

It's hard for a parent to hear retributions such as Lisa's and not take it personally. Reacting to the face value of this type of behavior is common and understandable. This is unacceptable behavior. Our culture tells us it must be punished. Many parents would think that taking time to understand where Lisa is coming from, hearing what she is trying to say to her father, is indulgent, permissive, and condones disrespectful behavior.

However, seeing Lisa's words and tone as his clue to her internal emotional state is exactly what is needed to build a bridge across a gap that is in present danger of widening. It is likely that her words hurt her father. Understandable. He may need some time to regain his balance and think about his next move before addressing the situation with her. Taking this needed time and walking away to prevent his emotional reaction does not mean he is letting her get away with it. He needs as long as it takes to approach her again and be able to respond with calmness and authority.

If their relationship is generally good and Lisa is reacting with an attitude she has picked up, he is better off to make light of it, answering something like, "Let me check my calendar. I believe it's the twenty-first century. Clearly we disagree about your wardrobe, clearly you are dressing the way you see fit, but your dear old dad is having a heart attack. Is there any way to help him out here?" He could add, "By the way, I didn't appreciate the characterization of lameness. Would you please tell me again that you didn't like my comment in a more respectful way."

However, if their relationship has been disconnected, chances are Lisa is reacting to many internal roots. If her father wants to mend some fences, he needs to take what she says to heart before asking for a change of attitude.

"Lisa, what you said to me last night about being lame...I've been thinking about it."

"Forget it, Dad."

"Yeah, but it didn't come out of nowhere. I want to know what it is I'm not getting and why you feel so angry with me. I guess I haven't been paying much attention lately to what's going on with you."

Even if he initially yelled and sent her to her room, these could be some of the most powerful words Lisa's father could say to her. They respect her integrity, her need for his attention, and they let her know that her feelings and opinions are important to him. He has built a bridge across the gap and given Lisa a safe way to approach him with her concerns and complaints. Whether she does or not is the risk he must be willing to take. He may be laying himself open to a barrage of criticisms and angry remarks. Most parents are not willing to make themselves vulnerable to this kind of risk. But if his words are said with genuine concern and compassion, he could have a fruitful discussion and learn some things about his daughter. If dismissal and punishment has been his game for a long time, a risk like this could be the most healing thing he could do. Likely it would take a good deal more than saying a few words to regain trust with his daughter, but it would be a great start.

Lisa may also dismiss him with, "Dad, get over it. It's no big deal." But his attempt at connection will still land with her. Once connection has been made, he may want to add that he does not appreciate being called names with such attitude and hopes that from now on she can say something more respectful even if it is a complaint. This will depend on how well the roots have been attended. If her need (for power, respect, or acceptance) has been addressed, calling her on her behavior is probably unnecessary.

The cumulative effect of a self-involved parent attending only to his own agenda can result in sending unintentional messages to his child that she is a nuisance, an inconvenience, invisible, even worthless. These messages remain in her internal emotional state and become the roots for future behavior, decisions, and choices. When connections allow opinions to be expressed between parent and child, there is no added baggage for the child to carry about invisibility or lack of importance.

Parents often need to swallow their pride, sometimes lose face, and pay attention to the messages they may be sending with their reactions.

> *Coming down off a righteous pedestal to apologize, to say I see it differently now and I wish I hadn't said what I did, is not being inconsistent and wishy-washy. On the contrary, it is the powerful thing to do.*

Think what those words would feel like coming from your parent even thirty or forty years after the fact.

When Behavior Gets Dramatic

If we do not pay attention, play detective, and get to the roots of our children's misbehavior, they have no choice but to get louder and more dramatic with their behavior. In *The Body Never Lies: The Lingering Effects of Hurtful Parenting*, Swiss psychologist Alice Miller says, "The original negative emotion is an important signal emitted by the body. If that message is ignored, the body has to emit new signals in an attempt to make itself heard." You may suddenly see hitting where there was none before or hear swearing or dramatic language like, "You're stupid," or "You hate me," or "I wish I was dead." It will be whatever the child thinks will get your attention.

Nine-year-old Brian started coming up with an attitude and rough words whenever his father asked him to do something he didn't want to. This behavior always got his father's negative attention. Tom was sure his son was tormenting him on purpose, so of course he wanted to stop him. When I suggested that he think of Brian's attitude as his clue to a deeper need, Tom was dubious. Through talking it out, it became apparent that Brian wanted more of his father, who worked long hours, was often away on business, and usually hid behind a newspaper when he was home. Whenever they did an activity together, Brian was a happy boy.

I suggested that whenever Tom heard the attitude or dramatic words, to go to his son and give him some positive attention.

"Isn't that rewarding bad behavior?" Tom asked. "I'd be giving him positive attention for negative behavior." It felt counterintuitive to Tom, whose logic told him to punish.

"That's if you see the attitude as what you are giving attention to," I said. "But in fact, when you have detected his need for connection with you, it is the *need* you are giving attention to. You are simply using the attitude as your clue. Put the clue aside, at least temporarily, and attend to the roots."

Indeed, Brian responded remarkably well to his father's experiment. The attitude has lessened, but when it emerges, Tom sees it as his kick in the pants.

The Basic Needs of a Child:

- **Respect:** To be respected as much as any other member of the family

- **Power:** To have a sense of personal power and capability to make something happen
- **Acceptance:** To be fully and unconditionally accepted for the person he is
- **Trust:** To be trusted and have the opportunity to trust others
- **Belonging:** To feel like an important, cared-about member of the family
- **Structure:** To be given strong and consistent guidelines in order to know what to expect and what is expected of him
- **Boundaries:** To have healthy boundaries in order to know the difference between the child's and the parent's responsibilities
- **Modeling:** To have positive, caring models

Translating "Childology"

Sometimes young children say things they don't mean because they don't understand the definition of words the way we do. It is important to address the root because you may be taking your child literally when she is trying to tell you something completely different.

Sharon complained about her four-year-old daughter Erica who claimed her mother was calling her "stupid" when in fact she wasn't at all. Later Erica said, "You think I'm stupid," and still later, "I'm stupid." Sharon talked at length in our parenting group about how Erica got on her nerves and infuriated her, how much they butted heads, and how regretful she was about some of the things she had said to her. But she had never called her stupid. She thought quite the opposite actually. Sharon answered Erica with, "You are not stupid. I never said that. I think you're very smart."

Since the incidents were still happening, it seemed clear that Sharon's response was not addressing what Erica was trying to tell her. I suggested that she ask Erica what the word stupid means to her the next time she heard it. Sure enough, when she asked Erica what stupid meant, she said, "When someone's angry at you, that means they think you're stupid." Her definition is not at all the opposite of smart. Her definition is "bad." Someone who is yelled at a lot is "stupid."

Think about it. If you are a young child and the most important person in your life is angry with you a fair amount of the time, wouldn't you think you were stupid or something was wrong with you? Erica may feel stupid for not knowing what to do to prevent her mother's anger.

Children don't question the adults in their life; they question themselves. They take in messages about themselves from what we say and do and either adapt, taking responsibility for our words and actions, or resist and rebel.

When our buttons get pushed, we react. Our perfectly good intentions go down the drain and the message received by our child is often far from what we intended. Sharon's angry reactions to her strong-willed child were intended to get her daughter to give her a moment's peace. But the message received was, *I'm stupid.*

Many of the words and phrases of young children require translation to understand their meaning in order to get at the roots. When we react in anger and accusation, children quickly learn how to get our attention and push our buttons. Relatively innocuous words can turn into powerful weapons. We may not like what they say, but when we can reflect back their meaning, rather than react to the face value, they eventually learn to say what they mean, because they trust we are listening.

The following is a chart with examples of a few dramatic words that children have learned will get a rise, together with a more appropriate way to respond.

Childology

Words We Hear	Meaning	Effective Response
I hate you.	I'm really, really mad at you.	You're really, really mad at me.
You love him more.	It's not fair.	It doesn't seem fair to you that he got to…
You're not my mommy.	This isn't what I expect from you.	You wish I would say something different.
You're mean.	I don't like what you just did/said.	You don't like it when I…
You don't love me.	You're not being fair. I can't get you to pay attention to me.	It doesn't feel fair to you that I'm spending so much time with the baby.
You can't make me.	You're taking my power away.	You wish you could do it the way you want.
You're stupid.	You don't understand me.	I wonder if you think I'm not hearing you.
I don't care. So what. (laughing)	I'm protecting myself from you.	You must think I'm nagging/being unfair.
I'm going to kill myself/ I wish I were dead.	It feels like nobody cares.	You must be feeling really hopeless.

Note: A statement like "I'm going to kill myself" or "I wish I were dead" should not be taken lightly, but often it is used for dramatic effect. An effective response is absolutely necessary to engage your child in a conversation so you can find out how serious the meaning is.

Self-Protective Behaviors

When children feel blamed or worry they are going to get in trouble or disappoint us, they have no option other than to defend and protect themselves. They run off, cover their ears, laugh, lie, blame someone else—anything to not get in trouble.

Lying is a child's defense mechanism that says,
I can't tell you the truth because you'll be mad.

Author Art Smith says in his Dad's survival manual, *Dadswork,* "Children learn to lie when they think they are responsible for how you feel. So they may say things that will keep you from getting upset, from worrying, from getting angry, from hitting them, from being disappointed in them." The word "lie" needs never be uttered, especially with a child under six. They are not lying by adult definition but covering up, not telling the whole story, or creating a fantasy. When a child expects to be blamed, "I didn't do it" seems the most expedient way to avoid the problem.

When we label children, they learn to identify themselves with the label. Instead of, "You're lying," try, "That doesn't sound like the truth to me. You probably don't want me to know what happened, if you're afraid I'll be mad. Maybe just start with one part, and I promise to listen. I know that you want to tell me the truth. Would it help to tell someone else first?"

Additional Obstacles

Often our children's obstacles are out of our control and require more than parent detective work. Many require professional consulting or diagnosing from herbalists to psychiatrists. Hormonal and other chemical imbalances can be the cause of continued explosive episodes, severe behaviors, and depression or serious lethargy. Poor nutrition can affect the child's level of activity or attentiveness. Brain wiring strongly affects learning processes. Temperamentally shy children can experience a great deal more anxiety than the more outgoing child. The list goes on. Stress factors always exacerbate any feature, genetic or otherwise, so regardless of the origin of the child's obstacle, the quality of your interaction means a great deal.

Main Ideas from Chapter 2:

- Behavior is your clue to your child's internal emotional state.
- Misbehavior is a red flag. Children don't misbehave on purpose but because something is preventing them from getting it right. There is always a reason, a trigger beneath inappropriate behavior.
- Misbehavior is like weeds in a garden. Ignoring its roots means the behavior will return.
- Punishing misbehavior only creates more conflict and stress for the child to fight against, requiring more punishment—a never-ending cycle.
- Punishments are external controls that deter the development of internal controls of right and wrong.
- When children feel unheard, words or behavior become loud and dramatic.
- Children's words often need interpretation to understand the meaning and not react to their face value.

Practice:

- Hold the thought: *My child wants to be successful so something must be in his way. What can that be and how can I help?* Remember, you will need to feel understanding or compassion, not anger, in order to help.
- Whenever your child is behaving in a way you don't like, ask yourself where this behavior is coming from, what is it trying to say, and what are its roots.

- When your child does something inappropriate, name the behavior with a line beneath to represent the surface of the ground. Draw lines going down into the soil to represent roots. Write something on each "root" that could be a cause of the behavior.

You could also make a chart like this:

Interpreting Behavior

Child's Behavior	Child's Emotions	Root
He threw his toy across the room and it broke.	Anger, frustration	He was mad that I told him to put his toys away. He didn't like my angry tone and was telling me that he wasn't being bad—he just wanted to keep playing.
She didn't do her homework and had to stay in for recess. Then she acted like it was all my fault.	She probably felt furious at the school and mad at me for getting angry with her.	She feels dumb and no one can help her find her way of working.

Check it out with your child. After the incident, tell your child you were thinking about what happened and wanted to find out if what you thought she meant was right.

CHAPTER 3

The Third Principle: My Child's Greatest Need Is Acceptance

B ecause my children are so different from one another, I had to learn to question my assumptions and expectations about their behavior and what they each needed from me, understanding that neither of their temperaments was right or wrong. When my daughter was born four-and-a-half years after my son, I literally had to start over. The expectations I held for my son did not fit my daughter. Her behavior was a complete mystery to me. She brought me to my knees and taught me how difficult this job of parenting really is. I had to learn to listen to my children rather than to the myriad voices around me. That meant paying attention. I learned that who they are was already there. We didn't have much to do with it. But my husband and I had everything to do with what directions their temperaments took. The hardest thing for me to learn was to stand back and trust—and to make sure my needs got met as well.

My son was the easygoing, extroverted, happy-go-lucky, social kid who made me feel like a fabulous parent. My daughter wanted it her way, put up a fight until things felt fair, looked at the world through a serious lens, didn't express her feelings readily, and was a one-friend-at-a-time girl. She made me question everything I thought I knew. Casey was adjustable wherever we went; Molly dug in her heels and didn't like change. My son's perception of the world seems to me widespread and accommodating, my daughter's has strict standards and delves to depths I can't begin to touch. They needed different aspects of me, and my job was to come up with what they needed without sacrificing myself.

It would have made life easier to use my accommodating son to compensate for my daughter. "Just let her have it," was the phrase I made sure I never used. Casey would have accommodated, but I knew he would have resented her for it. I would have been justified in many eyes to use punitive tactics with my daughter to get her to give up her fight, but then I would have raised a monster. Both were challenges and tried my patience. But I did not try to make them any different from who they are. Both are strong and secure and have always had respect and love for each other.

Unconditional Acceptance

Unconditional love is the right of every child.

Acceptance of the whole child is essential to nurturing each child's potential.

Sounds good, but how many of us really know what that means? Chances are if you experienced unconditional love and acceptance as a child, you understand—probably you don't even question it. Unfortunately few of us did, which makes it harder to give it to our children. To determine the amount of unconditional love you received, ask yourself:

- Did I believe that I would be loved and accepted no matter what?
Or
- Was I afraid that if I didn't behave a certain way I would be a disappointment?
- Did my opinions and beliefs matter to my parents?
Or

- Did I learn that what mattered to me, did not matter to my parents?
- Was I free to seek what I wanted in life?

Or

- Was it clear that I needed to make my parents proud and follow a path they wanted?

Acceptance is even more important to a child's healthy development than love. We can love our children but not accept them. But it is hard to wholly accept our children without loving them. Unconditional love requires acceptance of this individual being and what he brings to the world no matter what the temperament, type of energy, brain circuitry, learning style, gender, or hair color.

Acceptance means that my child does not have to be like me or think like me—or his brother. He is free to have his own needs and to hold different perceptions, beliefs, and opinions.

He may need to live a very different life than the rest of the family. Too many children give up when they know they will never live up to their parents' expectations, or they keep trying for that illusive approval by doing what they think they should instead of what they want. Either choice cripples potential.

What Will People Think?

When parents care more about what grandparents, in-laws, and even total strangers would say than what their child needs, *What will they think?* becomes the fear that blocks unconditional acceptance. The pressure is on to raise children society approves of—whatever the parent's interpretation. What it boils down to is that parents take their children's behavior personally and view it as a reflection of themselves. The almighty *They* determines their self-worth. Under that pressure, parents exert control over their children's thinking and behaving in order to gain *Their* approval—even though that approval might not be in the best interest of their child. Parents who fear criticism or ridicule by friends and family often misunderstand many children who are on the outside edges of the temperament continuum—impulsive or aggressive behavior or shy and withdrawn qualities.

The children who have the best chance of positively contributing to society are those whose unique potential has been allowed to blossom.

The children who are supported and accepted as they are, while disciplined to live respectfully within a community, will be our greatest assets. But when parents feel bound to parent as others think they should, they become trapped, and their children lose out. The strong-willed children will fight that control, push their buttons, and provoke daily power struggles to defend themselves against being pressured into someone they are not. And the easygoing, adaptable children will succumb to the pressure, do as their parents wish, and lose their own way.

"Bad" kids are usually the product of confused, exhausted, frustrated parents under pressure. Fearing what will become of their children, they try everything inconsistently before giving up. Instead, we need to change course, use a different parenting language than we are used to, and trust our children's individuality. It is essential for parents to understand that years of scientific evidence concludes that we as parents can only influence—never change—genetic, inborn personality traits. In *Nurture the Nature*, Michael Gurian says that "studies now show that personality and temperament (including whether a child is extroverted or introverted, aggressive or shy); styles of walking, talking, and running; even physical and mental strengths and disorders are in large part inborn." He sites the National Institute of Mental Health as having discovered "genetically activated brain mechanisms that are responsible for children's social behavior."

Every inherited trait is activated differently within each child's genetic system to create the amazing individual uniqueness of the human race. We as parents can help or hinder our children's path to success, but we cannot pave it. It is there at birth.

> *Individual success must not be measured by how well*
> *a child complies with the values of the adult world,*
> *but by how well the child's individual qualities and*
> *attributes are accepted and find purpose in that world.*

It begins with acceptance in the family.

The "I've Tried Everything and Nothing Works" Parent

Kristen was at her wit's end with ten-year-old Josh. She described him as a mostly loving, funny, independent kid who really wants to get life right but wants everyone to see things his way. He has a quick temper that he takes out on everyone in the family. "He's vicious to his little brother, fantastically rude, shouts at everyone, and most alarming, has recently started to use physical violence, throwing things at people and actually frightening me," Kristen said. "He's very big for ten. I am very frightened of violently expressed anger. He has actually said that he enjoys seeing me scared. He hits me and tells me to shut up. When I try to discipline him or tell him he can't hit his brother or me or say these awful things he becomes enraged. I've tried everything and nothing works—from ignoring him to grounding him to direct confrontation and screaming at him to physically pushing him out of the room," Kristen complained, really believing there was nothing left to do.

The problem is that Kristen's "everything" is either control or withdrawal, nothing in between. It's hard to see the behavior of a child like Josh as a signal to a deeper need crying out to be heard. When violence is the child's outcry, a parent's temptation is to retaliate and meet it head on, stopping it at all costs. There are no attempts to understand what he is trying to say. Josh's only choice is to keep on with louder and more dramatic behavior. His parents can only focus on his misbehavior so he doesn't know how to change.

Josh is learning that he is a problem. He likely feels afraid of his angry and aggressive impulses, since his parents have always rejected them, so he uses them as protection. Saying that he enjoys seeing his mother scared is most likely a defense—his protection against revealing his pain. He can't lose face at this point in his game, admit that he is hurting, or that what he wants most is his parent's love and acceptance. Perhaps he thinks if he takes the controlling position, he can avoid being controlled.

Josh needs to be believed in and trusted even more now than ever. He has gotten off track and needs a great deal of help getting back on. Kristen needs assurance that violence is not the track he wants to be on even though it may look that way. Sometimes it requires a leap of faith, to turn things around.

Learning to Accept

Josh is not so far off track yet that his mother has not been able to describe him as funny, loving, and independent. Aggressive tendencies in a child are often difficult to accept because we typically project or catastrophize them into fights, school detentions, jail sentences, and serial killings in a split second! But aggressiveness, when guided with acceptance and rechanneling the physical aspects, can be a positive characteristic. Society's most influential and powerful people did not reach their goals with smiles and kindness alone.

We cannot determine our child's temperament and potential,
nor can we change it. We can, however, influence
it strongly and even determine the direction it will take.

Acceptance is the best nourishment we can give. But when we think our children's future is our responsibility to determine, we must control it—an impossible task and a never-ending source of frustration and exhaustion.

Josh's parents need a new perspective on aggressiveness. They must set their expectations for a child who has a lot of angry energy that needs acceptable channeling, not for a child who is calm and submissive. To begin, they need to simply protect themselves, him, and anyone or anything else from harm, saying as little as possible during his outbursts. After the outburst, the roots need attending. A response could be, "You seem furious I am even here today. You must be very frustrated by what I am saying. Life must look pretty bad to you right now." This acknowledges his anger instead of raging at it or being cowed by it. When Josh screams at his mother to shut up, the best thing to do is wait out his storm as neutrally as possible and talk to him when he is calmer. Nothing can be accomplished when a child or a parent is in high gear. Kristen must wait for a window of opportunity to connect, to find something to put positive focus on, and to appeal to his hurting self.

She can focus on his aggression and determination in a positive way when it is not being used hurtfully. "Josh, you have such strong ideas of how things should be. Even though it makes life frustrating for you and probably always will, I have no doubt you will use your ideas to make something wonderful happen someday. The world needs your kind of mind." Chapter 6 will explore more ways a child's aggression and determination can be focused on positively.

His parents need to see Josh as that loving, funny, independent boy more often who is presently expressing his frustration through anger and physical aggression. When they see him that way, he will too. It's a shift in perception that brings about compassion for the hurt child inside. Whenever that funny, loving kid shows up, that is the time to give lots of positive loving notice, physical affection, and connection.

Acceptance as Mirroring

When our children are not doing as we ask, appear resistant at every turn, and become manipulative and sneaky, it's difficult to acknowledge that it may be us and the messages we are sending that require change. Instead we see disrespect, disobedience, rudeness, and defiance.

> Our children determine their identities by seeing themselves as we see them. We are their mirrors.

If what they see is *troublemaker, brat, disappointment, monster, dumb, violent, lazy,* their particular temperament will either submit to that perception or fight it every step of the way. The problem is that the more they fight, the more we perceive them negatively and the less we are able to understand their behavioral clues.

Every child deserves a mirror that reflects her greatness, her uniqueness, her most positive attributes. The child identifies herself with the attributes she sees reflected and doesn't question the mirror, only herself.

EYES LIKE WATER

Imagine your eyes like the surface of water. When you are calm, seeing your child with the perspectives presented here, your eyes are like still water. In that stillness, your child can see himself clearly. He sees who he really is. But when fear, anger, resentment, or other reactive emotions take over, your eyes become like water in a storm with rough waves and white caps. Your child cannot see himself in that turbulent water; what he sees is turbulence.

Dorothy had to call on all her patience to parent her five-year-old daughter, who always needed things to be just so. Sophie's perfectionism meant that she was slow and methodical and rarely would change how she did anything once she got it the way she liked it. Dorothy was often on Sophie's case to "just hurry it up. It doesn't matter if you write every letter with a different color. You're taking forever, and I don't have the time for this." Dorothy assumed that Sophie refused to try any other way and was trying to make her mother mad. Dorothy was on edge whenever Sophie got involved in one of her projects.

Dorothy shared in our class one day that she thought Sophie was afraid to try anything new in case it wouldn't turn out to be what she envisioned. She feared that Sophie's stubbornness to change her ways would cause her trouble in school and on down the line. She wished that Sophie would just ease up, let things go, and be a kid. She would often tell her, "Just let it roll off your back, Soph. You'll be much happier that way." But Dorothy didn't understand what made Sophie happy.

After discussing this problem in class, Dorothy realized she was not accepting Sophie's intense attention to detail as part of her temperament and personality. She thought with effort she could get Sophie to change.

I told Dorothy to ask Sophie what she would want to change about herself if she could. Sophie initially said she wished she were six and could fly. Then she said that she would want ten arms, four sets of eyes, and one mouth. She said that they would help her be faster and not lazy.

"You could have hit me with a ton of bricks and it would not have been as big a blow as the realization that I'd been sending out the message that she was lazy!" Dorothy expressed to us. "She then went on to tell me that if she had ten arms, she could just write and write and write and all the words would be perfect. She said that her brain has so much it wants to do, but her body was just too 'lazy,' as she put it again."

Then Dorothy asked Sophie what she would not want to change about herself. She said that she would always want to be colorful, "because I love rainbows so much!" and that using one color all the time was boring and lazy (there's that word again) and that using a different color for every letter in a word was "exciting" to her.

"That's when I realized that the end result is of no importance to her," Dorothy said. "It's all about the process. She had to find her own way to make it more interesting and colorful and that's what made her happy."

Dorothy described her realization as a turning point in their relationship. By shifting her perception from what she thought was a negative to seeing it as a positive, she realized what a gift Sophie possesses. Dorothy soon began presenting a very different mirror for her daughter to look into. "Lazy" left her vocabulary and her perception.

"Different" Children

The children who push our buttons are usually children who are temperamentally more difficult to handle. They can be opposite from us in nature or scarily like us. They threaten our sense of ourselves—who we have learned to be. They disrupt our lives, cause us severe inconvenience, and lead us to question why we ever had children. They force us to look at our buttons and our reactions and demand that we work at this parenting business. They are indeed different, but they need us to know that "different" doesn't mean wrong. They often experience pain because our cultural system, especially our educational system, doesn't always understand them.

These children are trying to tell us that square pegs cannot fit into round holes.

Samantha reported that she was having difficulty getting seven-year-old Ethan to read the books his teacher required. "When I tell him it's time to read," Samantha bemoaned, "He shouts at me, says 'I'm not doing it,' and runs off. If we sit down together to read he fidgets, makes wild guesses, blows raspberries, fiddles with things, or stares into space." Intending to motivate him to read, Samantha threatened Ethan with writing in his reading journal that he refused to finish his book.

Threats do not work with children who don't like being told what to do. Ethan shouted back that he didn't care and was going to rip up the book. As soon as he grabbed the book, Samantha realized what she had provoked. Fortunately she had learned how to shift gears. She regrouped, breathed deeply, and stepped out of the power struggle.

Putting her hands on the book to protect it, Samantha said, "Ethan I wonder if Mrs. Kaveney has picked the wrong book for you. I don't think we should read anymore until I talk to her about it. This book doesn't interest you. I'm sorry that I was forcing you to read it." Ethan's whole body relaxed. He let go of the book and said simply, "Okay," and got ready for bed.

Samantha was hesitant about questioning a teacher's decisions but suggested that the books Ethan was being asked to read were too difficult for him. Wanting more success with Ethan herself, his teacher tried a book from a lower level of reading skill. Samantha reported that Ethan is a different child. She saw clearly that his behavior was not defiant but was the result of feeling unsuccessful. The stress of not being able to keep up with his classmates had been provoking his reactive, angry, sometimes destructive behavior that he took out on his mother, the person with whom he felt safest.

"Now he sits happily with me for reading, and I've even caught him reading to his little sister. When he's not sure he guesses at words instead of getting angry and running off. I can see the sense of accomplishment on his face. He even wants to play spelling games on the way to school now."

This may sound too good to be true, but it is indeed a true story. Samantha had already learned the language that Ethan responded to. But everything in a child's life presents a new learning curve. She was being influenced by what his teacher was expecting of him rather than listening to his frustrated behavior signals. When she did, she could accept his differences. Ethan's learning style is different from other boys his age. So many children have it much worse than Ethan within a system that doesn't always fit the child's learning style. When we see these children as resistant and oppositional, we all lose. When we see that they need something different and that it is not their fault, the search alone will help them feel more accepted.

Lessons from a Strong-Willed Child

Sometimes we get our priorities confused, especially when our buttons get pushed. Much of the time we just want our children to listen and do what we say so we can feel like competent parents. We justify this desire with the societal belief that children need to learn to do what they are told because that's how it will be in the big world. Unintentionally we create problems when we come up against children who are strong-willed, persistent, sensitive, and unpredictable. Remember, they too want to be successful and to please us—just not in the way we are asking.

There is nothing wrong with a child who doesn't like being told what to do. His resistance does not mean he is obstinate and disrespectful. He is simply sensitive to feeling discounted when his parent says, "You have to do what I say."

When he says, "No I don't," he means, "I don't like being talked to that way. I need to understand why I have to do it your way. I can do it when it makes logical sense to me."

My daughter Molly gave me a run for my money for the first seven years of her life. I finally understood and gradually was able to accept her as I learned who she was and what she needed. My learning process took years.

Her difficulty with change and transition made our move from New York City to small-town New Hampshire tough for her. We assumed that at age three she would forget New York by the end of the first week in New Hampshire, but it took two years before New York and New Hampshire were even on the same par.

The Christmas of Molly's fifth year and our second year in New Hampshire, Molly had just begun to settle into her new life. Shortly before Christmas while she was at preschool, her father and I put the Christmas tree in its stand and strung the lights. Being only our second Christmas in the new house, our traditions were not set, and we decided to put the tree in front of the window instead of across the room where it had been the year before. When Molly came home, I ushered her into the living room anticipating her excitement. In a sudden burst of tears, she blurted out, "It's not Christmas! It can't go there, it has to go over there! You have to move it." Her fragile new picture of Christmas had been destroyed. She couldn't make the leap to what we perceived as an improvement like her ten-year-old brother could. Her mind worked differently, and it challenged us daily.

It would have been easy to say either, "Tough, Moll, this is what the rest of us want," or "Okay, we'll move it. Just don't get so upset," but the fallout would have been great either way. If we had moved the tree to make her happy, the rest of us would have felt victimized by her temperament and resentful of her power. If I had told her it's three against one, she would have held onto the injustice and made our lives miserable. It had to be a win/win.

Fortunately, I had learned enough about her to know that she was not being defiant or oppositional, she was simply having a hard time coping with the stress of change.

Had I not learned this, she would have borne the brunt of my frustrated wrath as had often been the case previously. Instead, I took a few deep breaths to shift gears and put my arms around her.

"So moving the Christmas tree makes it not seem like Christmas to you," I said patiently, not having the faintest idea what my next move would be.

"Yes! You can't do that. You *have* to move it back." I held her and let the tears come.

Buying myself some time, I said, "You know what. I really understand why it feels wrong to you. Last Christmas it was different. Let's wait until the end of the day when we can talk about this with Poppy and Casey. Let's go do something else now."

Molly trusted from past experience that it would not be forgotten and knew that her feelings were taken into account, so she was able to leave the living room. Had it been otherwise, I imagine she would have thrown a major tantrum right there, especially if she thought it would get me to move the tree. I had also learned that she would not forget about it, and I couldn't just sweep the issue under the carpet and hope for the best.

We all discussed the tree, and the rest of us clearly wanted it to remain in front of the window. We did some negotiating about her picking out the tree the next year or putting colored lights on instead of the all-white, but she still was not sold. That evening we happened to drive by the front of the house. The lights from the Christmas tree sparkled in the front window. I said, "Look, Molly. Look at the lights in the window." We all oohed and aahed—Molly included. She agreed with the rest of us that the tree should stay.

Because she trusted we would find a resolution, she had no reason to put up a defense. Feeling understood went a long way toward helping her cope with the change. Otherwise she wouldn't have agreed even if she liked the way the lights looked in the window. She wanted to cooperate, but she had to find her own way to do it. It had to make sense to her.

Making Adjustments for the Distractible Child

Seven-year-old Jackson is impulsive and distractible. He has a hard time sitting still and often makes loud, silly noises when he is bored or unstructured. But take him to the reptile house at the zoo, and you can't tear him away. It is of course impossible and exhausting for most parents to engage their children's interests at all times, but knowing that distractible brains can completely focus when they are engaged and interested helps parents feel hopeful.

Jackson's music class was to be part of the first and second grade recital. There were about eighty children involved. The first graders were to sing a few songs then sit to the side while the second graders performed before combining for the finale—a situation ripe for a distractible child to misbehave. They practiced for weeks and Jackson was excited as the recital drew near.

His parents had learned a lot about his behavior, but Jackson had been a constant challenge for them. They had come a long way from seeing Jackson as being a problem and misbehaving on purpose to understanding the obstacle he has to work with.

As the recital grew close Jon assured his son that they would be right there to support him and knew he would do a beautiful job. On the day of the recital, Jon took a dollar bill from his wallet and gave it to his son saying, "This is a 'buck for good luck.' Keep it in your shirtsleeve and think about it if you feel uncomfortable. If you start to think you can't go on, hold onto it tightly in your hand. Then if you know you've had enough, raise the hand with the dollar in it, and one of us will help you off the stage." Jon was setting his expectations for success.

Jackson did succeed in the recital. The dollar bill was tightly crumpled in his fist, and his parents congratulated him on what he had accomplished with his own effort. When he had something tangible to focus on, Jackson was able to stay on target longer than usual.

The Roles of Fear and Doubt

When we can see behavior as an expression of our children's internal state, we can help them cope with their individual struggles, even if we never completely understand what they are. If we truly believe that they want to be successful and are unique and capable in their own way, our fears for their future will diminish. Because we are in charge of these very powerful human beings, we as parents can rarely rid ourselves of fear entirely. It is the hazard of the profession. However, we can own our fear without letting it parent our children.

> When fear drives our parenting, it prevents us from connecting and knowing our child. It keeps us stuck in our heads, in the past or the future, unable to hear what our child hears. It keeps us in reaction.

Doubt, on the other hand, is the barometer by which we can tell whether we are being flexible or inflexible. We all know parents who are cocksure of their parenting; no one can tell them what to do. Not one of us would want to be their child. Unfortunately many of us were.

> Doubt keeps us conscious and proactive. Doubt keeps us searching and learning. It keeps us on our toes, unable to dip into complacency and neglect. It allows for mistakes, apologies, and ongoing communication.

We will always wonder what to do or if we did the right thing. We all have a line, bendable and sometimes fuzzy, on either side of which we will always teeter. It is the mark of a conscientious parent to be unsure which side of the line to defer to. As long as we don't hold rigidly to the line or fall far from it, we can be sure we are paying attention.

Main Ideas from Chapter 3:

- A child's temperament is inborn. It cannot be changed but can be greatly influenced by a parent both positively and negatively.
- Acceptance of the whole child is more powerful even than love.
- Accepting the child is fundamental to making connection and influencing behavior positively.
- Acceptance of the child does not mean acceptance of the behavior.
- Children build their identities on the reflection they see of themselves in their parents' eyes.
- The children most difficult to handle pose threats because they are either opposite in nature or very much like their parent.
- Button-pushing children teach parents what they most need to learn.
- Strong-willed children want to cooperate—but not always in the way we want them to.
- Fear keeps us stuck. Doubt keeps us conscious.

Practice:

- List your child's unique personality characteristics. (You may want to use the temperament charts in Mary Sheedy Kurcinka's *Raising Your Spirited Child*.) Put a plus sign next to the ones that you like about your child, a checkmark next to the ones you find difficult to manage, and a minus sign next to the ones you have concerns about. Each may have more than one mark.

1. List one or two parenting methods that help with the ones checkmarked.
2. Write one positive aspect about the ones marked with a minus.

- In what areas, if any you can see now, could your child become competent?
- Write a paragraph or two about your child's individual capabilities. Read it when you are frustrated with her behavior.
- How well does your child's unique personality fit with your expectations of her?
- Do you more often find yourself expecting your child to do something wrong or to succeed, rise to an occasion, and be delightful or creative?
- Is your child accepted in his community—school, friends, relatives? If not, how can you help those perceptions to change?
- How would you feel if your child wants to do something in life that you do not approve of?

CHAPTER 4

The Fourth Principle: Expectations Must Be Set for Success

Hillary and her twelve-year-old daughter came to see me after Shannon had gotten into some difficult problems. She was lying to her mother about where she was after school and was hanging out with a boy who had already been in trouble with the police. Her mother was distraught. Shannon was tight-lipped until she blurted out, "I'm never good enough for you."

"Where did you ever get that?" Hillary said, "I have never said that!"

"You don't have to," Shannon said. "You expect me to be perfect. I'm not you, Mom. And I'm not Jess either. Why can't you just leave me alone?"

"I just want you to make good decisions, honey," Hillary pleaded.

"No, you want me to make the decisions you would make."

Over the years, Shannon's mother has unintentionally and unconsciously sent Shannon the message that *Your way isn't good enough. You don't quite get it right. Doing it my way would be better.* Hillary would never dream of saying anything like that to her daughter. It came directly from her unspoken, but clearly received, expectations.

Hillary had always thought it was her job to tell Shannon what to do so she would learn. She hadn't realized that she was expecting her very different daughter to be more like her. Fearing Shannon wouldn't get it right without her mother's prodding, Hillary had been erecting a wall of resistance in her younger daughter. Shannon's older sister Jess was a high achiever and, in Shannon's view, was the daughter her mother was proud of. Shannon assumed she was a disappointment and was starting to turn away.

When a child is resistant to requests or demands, becomes parent-deaf, or an attitude accompanies sarcastic remarks, parents panic fearing their child will never succeed or measure up to what the world expects. Most want to enforce compliance and "proper behavior," and do so with coercive tactics. Adjusting expectations to fit the child seems counterproductive. It feels too risky to address what the child needs rather than what society or the in-laws expect.

Meeting certain parental expectations is often difficult or impossible for many children. Fear of our child's failure or unhappiness leads us to operate from the outside in. We want our children to the meet the expectations by which we were raised, and so often set inappropriate expectations for many of our children. We set them with all the best intentions but inadvertently prevent them from discovering their own way and encourage dependence on us or someone else—often leading to bad decision making.

The Definition of Success

As defined in Chapter 1, success indicates a child in balance with his world and with himself. He knows he is okay the way he is without sacrificing any part of his nature to win praise or approval. His internal emotional state is calm even though his energy level may be high. When expectations are set for success, the child's development is understood, temperamental characteristics are accepted, and he can develop confidence in himself so his unique talents and abilities can flourish.

The principles presented in this book support the belief that each child is born perfect—no matter what the learning style or handicap—and has come to us, whether by birth or adoption, for the purpose of our mutual learning. When we demand that our children do it our way, we pull them off balance and plant obstacles in their path in an attempt to make ourselves feel or look better.

That said, children's impulses and choices often get them into difficult situations. They can be annoying and cause problems for others due to their egocentric and self-serving natures. They need structure, limits, and realistic expectations. They need to understand and respect the rights of others. A balance must be found.

The responsibility to influence children's behavior positively begins with the parent.

> *Children behave in the way they perceive they are expected to behave.*

Because Shannon saw disappointment reflected in her mother's eyes, she perceived that her mother expected her to be a disappointment—so she believed she would be a disappointment no matter what. Hillary needs to look at her daughter through a new lens, one that focuses on her capability rather than her inadequacy. To do this she must accept Shannon as she is, and she will then happily rise to meet a more positive view of herself where expectations are high but appropriate for Shannon.

High Expectations Are Often Unrealistic

Hillary thought that she was accepting Shannon, but her clue lies in Shannon's words and behaviors that tell her mother that something is wrong deep inside. Instead of insisting that Shannon is wrong to believe her mother wants perfection, Hillary needs to acknowledge Shannon's perception and look harder at what has been unconsciously set in place. A better response might be, "If you are getting from me that I want you to be somebody different, I need to look at that. Can we talk this through, and will you tell me if you don't think I'm hearing you?" With words like these, Shannon has little to fight against, and Hillary will find she has far more influence than when she was telling Shannon what to do.

> We must know our children's individual strengths and weaknesses
> and have a realistic view of them. Then we can support their
> own capabilities, rather than those we wish they had.

But when children think their parents want them to be someone else, someone better, easier, smarter, they may angrily resist and sometimes self-destruct.

Shannon is on the verge of adolescence. If she believes her mother wishes she were different, she will feel she doesn't belong and will look for a friend or group of friends who accept her for who she is. She will do whatever they want in order to belong. Her authority figure will switch to one who believes in her (or so she perceives)—our worst nightmare. When a child has spent years expected to do as she is told, she never has the opportunity to solve problems, think for herself, or learn to say no confidently.

Adjusting Expectations for Success

We not only expect certain behaviors from our children, but we expect certain attitudes to accompany those behaviors. *Not only do I expect my child to listen to me and do what I say, but I expect her to do it pleasantly, without complaints. Not only do I expect my child to do the dishes, but I also expect her to do them the way I would do them. I expect my son to clean his room, but I also expect him to want a clean room.* So even if they do what we want, we still set them up for failure if they don't do it the way we want. Wouldn't any child subject to such expectations end up feeling not quite good enough?

Our children have a right to their feelings and their own way of accomplishing things. If your child is grudgingly taking the trash out as you have asked while muttering under his breath something about the stupid trash and something about his stupid brother never doing anything, restrain yourself from commenting. Let it be enough that he is doing it.

Once children exhibit distressful behavior, expectations must adjust to what the child can be successful in meeting at the present time.

A young child who hits other children if they don't do what he wants should not be expected to suddenly stop hitting. He will learn far better with a parent who understands that his aggressive energy is very real and can help him rechannel that energy—hitting a pillow or punching bag, jumping on a trampoline, ripping up a drawing of who he is mad at, banging on a piano—rather than expecting the energy to disappear or the child to be able to stop it.

You know the expression *choose your battles*. Choose your expectations as well. Ask yourself whether the obstacle your child is experiencing is coming from your expectations, someone else's, the circumstance, or his internal emotional state which may be a cumulative collection of past experience—his own expectations. Children can be harder on themselves than we are. But that internal pressure comes from somewhere.

Remember, when you see inappropriate behavior, think, *My child is having a problem, not being a problem.*

Alan had a tough time when he felt overstimulated by events and people from the time he was little. At home, and one-on-one, he was fine, but in the supermarket, at birthday parties, and at preschool, he had a very hard time staying calm and behaving appropriately. He would hide behind his mother when people approached, often grabbed the birthday presents at parties, and sometimes hit other children or his teacher at preschool.

Barbara needed Alan, now five, to be polite and socially adept as had been expected of her. With each occurrence of difficult behavior, she would lecture Alan, telling him he had to be nice, say hello nicely, look someone in the eye and answer their questions—and certainly to stop hitting. As her expectations were met with even more aggressive attempts to push people away, Barbara's tactics became more controlling. She shouted, "You have got to learn to be polite. You can't be this way. It's perfectly easy. Just look at someone and say hello!" Or "When are you going to stop hitting. You're not a baby anymore." Alan's behavior evolved to grunting, sticking out his tongue at people, and even spitting.

One day when Barbara and Alan were in the supermarket, a loaded environment for him, a friend of Barbara's approached. As Barbara turned toward Alan with a hopefully expectant look, he grabbed her pocketbook from the shopping cart, swung it around and around above his head, and shouted nonsense words. Barbara was mortified.

"Your expectations may be unrealistic for him," I suggested.

"But isn't it important to set high expectations for our children?" Barbara asked.

"Absolutely," I answered, "as long as your child can be successful meeting them. Your expectations of socially proper behavior may set Alan up for failure, because he is not capable of meeting them right now. He is resisting what you want because he doesn't know how to do it. Start with where he is, and then as he becomes successful, you can gradually raise the bar."

I suggested that she begin by understanding and accepting her son's sensitive and easily overloaded temperament and set her expectations accordingly. For instance, it would be appropriate to expect that he will have a hard time in public, especially meeting people. And to expect that he will not be able to say hello easily, so she should say it for both of them. She can expect that he will feel uncomfortable and nervous, but she can also expect him to stand next to her quietly while she puts her arm around his shoulders for comfort.

"Oh, that's sounds so nice!" Barbara said. But she worried that that kind of response would condone Alan's behavior and give him permission to remain antisocial.

It takes an enormous amount of trust to witness a child's highly inappropriate behavior and pull back on your expectations instead of raising them higher or using punishment, reprimands, and lectures to control the results you want. Raising and coercing expectations only convinces the child further that he is unacceptable.

Alan was raising a huge red flag by swinging the pocketbook over his head. It was Barbara's clue to adjust her expectations. With more help she did, and Alan has since settled in to perfectly appropriate behavior at school and in his larger world where he is now doing quite well. His aggressive tendencies have mellowed since rechanneling his energy into sports. He has good friends and even speaks politely to Barbara's friends.

What Does My Child Think I Expect?

The value our children perceive we place on them is the value they place on themselves.

Children don't question our judgments, they question themselves. If I get angry with my four-year-old for grabbing a doll away from her friend, tell her she's being mean, and send her to her room to think about it, she will not think, *Next time I won't grab what my friend is playing with,* she will think that she has been bad. She won't have the maturity to detach and think, *Mommy is wrong about me. I'm not mean. I just wanted to have that doll.* But she might think, *I can't ever do it right. Mommy doesn't love me.* If we don't trust our children, they are likely to behave in an untrustworthy manner, but if we trust them and expect them to want to do the right thing, they will not want to betray that trust and will likely rise to the occasion.

Every Christmas, Eve makes magnificent gingerbread houses for her girls. They devour them over the next few days. This Christmas, Eve decided to make her own gingerbread house as well. She decorated it simply and beautifully with white frosting and a few almonds and put a candle inside. She was quite proud of it and placed it in a prominent spot in the kitchen.

Eve's nemesis, three-year-old Madison, began saying, "I'm going to eat your gingerbread house" every time she didn't get her way. Eve told Madison it was hers and was not for eating, but Madison's threats continued and Eve began to threaten back. One day an almond was missing from its front door. Shelly, Madison's older sister, told her mother that Madison had snitched it. Eve was livid but brought the issue to our class before saying anything to Madison. Eve described an ungrateful, disrespectful brat to us. She was to the point of tears over Madison's constant defiant behavior. "It's like she's punishing me," she said.

I asked Eve what she expected of Madison. She said emphatically, "To leave it alone, to respect that it is my special gingerbread house and to not eat it!" I suggested that Madison had actually met that expectation. Eve did not agree. "No, she didn't. She's after me all the time about it. Why can't she just cut it out?" I proposed to Eve that she was actually expecting Madison to do a good deal more—to actually ignore the house completely. If she was going to leave it in Madison's sight, her expectation amounted to minor torture for her three-year-old.

In order to change things around, Eve would have to change her perception of her daughter. She would need to see that Madison was *having* a problem, not *being* a problem, and adapt the situation for a three-year-old. The tears poured out as she heard the suggestions from the class—what deep down she already knew. The missing almond was Madison's final clue that she had come to the brink of her ability to control her impulses. If she had seen Madison's threats and then the missing almond as signals rather than acts of belligerence, Eve could have looked to the roots to see that Madison was just as frustrated as she was. There was even cause for congratulations for restraining herself that long. But Eve didn't recognize the behavior as clues and had set her daughter up to misbehave. Madison thought her mother saw her as bad, so she would have continued on that track. Her next step likely would have been smashing the gingerbread house.

Most of us in class thought that Eve should simply move the house out of sight, but after clarity and objectivity replaced Eve's blurred perception, she came up with a better idea. "I think I'll go home and suggest to Madison that we make another little gingerbread house to sit next to mine so they can be mother and daughter gingerbread houses. She'll love that."

The next week we found out that not only had that worked, but when Madison was out with her father, she bought a tiny ceramic sheep to put outside the front door of her mother's gingerbread house. Their two houses sat peacefully side by side until a week later when Madison gave in to her temptation and ate hers. Her mother's was no longer a problem for her.

When we focus only on our child's behavior, we often catastrophize that behavior to future crises and miss the opportunity to see what's really happening. If this focus continues throughout their development, and our fears and worries drive our parenting, we do our children a serious disservice.

Depression and rebellion are two avenues open to children who get the message again and again that they cannot meet up to what is expected of them.

Misunderstandings and miscommunication can lead to fulfillment of our greatest fears. We have all seen the end products. We just don't put the pieces together to understand where it begins.

A Child's Job Is to Get What He Wants When He Wants It

Children are always after what they want—it's normal. Actually, aren't we all? The older we get, the better we disguise it, but isn't that why we get so angry with our children—because they're not doing what we want? This does not mean we should give them what they want. But when we hold the expectation that they should not ask for, fight for, demand what they want, we are holding a very unrealistic expectation. Not only is it developmentally appropriate for a child to go after what he wants, but also when the child is made to believe he is bad for wanting, his developmental drive is thwarted, and he could develop narcissistic tendencies. When we fear something is going to be withheld from us or is no longer available, then when it is available, we hoard it or gorge on it. If a child is told over and over that he can't have what he wants, he will get more and more demanding.

If your child says, "I want to build a rocket," instead of, "Don't be silly. You can't do that," try instead, "How can you make that happen?" It is our fears that prompt the immediate, "No, you can't." The anger and frustration that often accompany recurrent demands tells children that we expect them to be satisfied without what they want. But we don't have to pay money, sacrifice our time, or spoil a child to address the want. The want is normal. We may not get it for them, but we can let them know their desire is understandable.

Dawn had warned her eleven-year-old, Jamie, that they were only getting a gift for her aunt when they entered the department store, but sure enough as soon as her back was turned, she heard, "Mom! I have to have this!" Dawn had spent years trying to teach Jamie that he couldn't always get what he wanted but felt she was in a losing battle. Once she understood this principle, she tried something new. She walked over to see the red, shiny remote control car that had caught his attention. Instead of ignoring his desire and telling him he couldn't have it, she said, "Boy, that's beautiful isn't it? I'm sure if I were you, I'd want that." Then she added, "I was in a store the other day and saw a chair I really wanted. I knew exactly where I'd put it in our living room. It was beautiful. But I couldn't afford it." He was amazed. She realized that he had never heard her talk about her desires or inability to buy something she wanted. They finished shopping and walked out of the store sharing stories about things they both wished for. She validated his desire—enough to allow him to move on—and he learned something about delayed gratification.

Children Will Rise to a Challenge When It Is Offered

Reacting to our children's behavior and taking it at face value can so easily lead us into power struggles and the cycle of worse and worse behavior.

We will stop the power struggles only when we stop ourselves from reacting.

Usually when we detect a problem, we move right into directing mode, telling our children what to do or what not to do. Many children will then feel controlled and resist; we react and battles ensue when they don't do what we want. Do we really expect them to back down and lose the battle willingly? Our easygoing, adaptable children might—actually we wouldn't engage in a battle with them anyway—but our strong-willed, persistent children definitely will not back down unless we fight hard enough to break them.

Amy has two girls, Olivia, five, and Emily, eight. Olivia is the button pusher. She is stubborn, bullheaded, and does not like to be told what to do. She and her mother butt heads regularly. Amy and I have been searching for what provokes her daughter's angry meltdowns so Amy can stop focusing on what a terrible mother she is long enough to see the obstacle in Olivia's way. Being able to step outside her own perspective and into her daughter's requires Amy to have a point of objectivity. When she is frustrated in her own work, exhausted from normal mothering duties, and thinks she hasn't a clue how to handle her daughter, her perspective narrows. She takes Olivia's behavior very personally. All she can think is, *What is wrong with her? What doesn't she understand about what I've asked her to do? She's ungrateful and inconsiderate*, and *She's screwing with me*.

Olivia and her older sister, Emily, were playing with the two boys who lived next door, one a year older and one a year younger than Emily. As usual, the three older children didn't want to do what Olivia wanted to do. Not one to back down and play what they wanted, Olivia tried different tactics to get them engaged with her but to no avail. Suddenly she dashed through the kitchen and headed up the back stairs when her mother stopped her, "You can't go up there. I just mopped the stairs."

Olivia cried, "I have to get my new game."

"You can get it in ten minutes when the stairs are dry," Amy said, expecting that Olivia should understand and cooperate. Instead, Olivia lost it. She screamed and cried that it wasn't fair, that she hated everybody, and that her life was terrible. Amy could only see that Olivia was being unreasonable and uncooperative, stuck in a world of her own, unable ever to be considerate of anyone else.

"What didn't she understand about the stairs being just cleaned?" Amy exclaimed to me. "I had just finished mopping the whole kitchen and the stairs and then she starts with this." Amy saw that her job as a mother was to teach Olivia to see the "right" way, and if she couldn't, there was something wrong with Olivia. As soon as I suggested that perhaps Olivia had a plan in mind that this game might be something all four of them would want to play and in her five-year-old brain she didn't have a minute to lose, Amy said, "I never thought of that. I'm sure you're right." If Amy could have understood the immediacy of Olivia's agenda and based her expectations on her daughter's intense determination, she might have been able to problem-solve instead of insight a riot. Instead, Amy's expectations were set for a child who would be able to see the hard work her mother had just put in, understand that her shoes would dirty the just-cleaned steps, and would step aside, apologize, and wait for ten minutes. Realistic?

Why is it as parents we don't stop and think? Why is it so hard to hold expectations that are appropriate? Don't we adore our kids and want only the best?

> It must be because we are afraid that if our expectations are
> not set for the people we hope our children to become,
> they will never become those people and end up
> failures—ourselves along with them.

So we focus on those illusive qualities we want to instill and ironically chip away at our children's self-confidence. We miss all kinds of teaching opportunities.

"Olivia, wait! I just mopped the stairs. How can you get upstairs without getting any dirt from your shoes on the clean steps?" This sets a challenge for Olivia rather than thwarting her plan. Being the highly spirited child she is, Olivia would have risen to that challenge, thought about the problem, and chosen any number of creative solutions from taking off her shoes and going up in her socks to putting plastic bags over her shoes to climbing up on her hands and knees.

But what if Amy wasn't that quick on her feet? What if she was still reactive, yet took time to think once the meltdown occurred? If Amy saw the meltdown as Olivia's uncontainable frustration due to her persistent nature instead of a lack of consideration, she could say, "Boy you really want to get to that game fast, don't you? You must have a plan in mind." Then she could ask Olivia how she could do it without getting the steps dirty.

For many, this might feel like backing down, giving in, rewarding bad behavior, and letting Olivia get away with her demands. But by stopping her reaction and adjusting her unrealistic expectation, Amy is in no way backing down or losing authority.

Saying what we mean and meaning what we say is one thing. But saying something unreasonable and then changing it to something reasonable is the smart thing to do.

Acknowledging Strengths and Weaknesses

Appropriate expectations need to be based on the characteristics and qualities of each person. We all have strengths and weaknesses, talents and quirks. Talk with your children about personality qualities. Ask them to judge their own.

- What do you think are your best qualities/strengths?
- What are the most difficult parts of your personality?
- Can you think of what you might learn from those difficult parts?
- What are the strengths and weaknesses of your siblings?
- What do you see as my best and worst qualities?
- What happens when we're both at our best? And both at our worst?

Rich discussions can come from thinking about what you all do well and what you don't. A relaxed acceptance of personal deficits allows children to be more tolerant of themselves and others and to see the humanness in everyone. It can be useful to talk to a child about her difficulty with shifts in plans, the roughness or prickliness of new clothes and tags, certain tastes, being quick to feel upset or scared. Then you can add how well she pays attention and focuses on what she is doing, how thoughtful she is toward others, or how easy it is for her to try new foods. Children need to know that their idiosyncrasies are normal, that we all have them, and that they are always balanced with attributes.

Our Children's Expectations of Themselves Can Be Too High

Children sometimes put more pressure on themselves than we do. They don't want to disappoint us—or anyone for that matter. This may lead some to being very "good," diligent, and working too hard at what they think will make everyone proud. The tension may cause physical illness, poor appetite or sleep, or a quick fuse on a child who is normally easygoing. When you see this self-imposed pressure, it may be time to intervene with a mental-health day from school and engage in something fun and relaxing. Evaluate your child's school performance. If he is doing well, be sure to pull way back on any performance-related expectations you may be imposing. Ask your child to evaluate all his activities and chose one or two to drop for the time being.

Chewing nails, pulling out hair, nervous ticks, head banging, stomachaches, and wetting the bed after a long time of control are all signs of stress. We have a myth that childhood is a stress-free time of life. It is not true. When children live under high expectations at the same time they are developing their own identities, almost everything has the potential of being confusing and frustrating for them. We need to give them a break and let them just be to play and hang out. They don't need to behave like little adults, to appreciate what we are doing for them, or to take on more activities than they can handle so we can be proud of them.

When expectations are set appropriately, our children will feel good about themselves, confident of their abilities, accepting of

Confident Parents, Remarkable Kids

their inabilities, relaxed, and fun to be with. They will feel balanced and successful.

Main Ideas from Chapter 4:

- Unspoken, unexamined expectations set many children up for failure. They are usually set for the child you want.
- Children behave in the way they *perceive* they are expected to behave.
- Setting expectations for successful behavior means beginning with adjusting expectations for what is happening in the present.
- Children who don't believe they can live up to what their parents expect of them often rebel or become depressed.
- A child's job is to get what he wants when he wants it. Giving it may be inappropriate, but expecting otherwise is unrealistic.
- We can acknowledge a child's want without sacrificing time, spending money, or spoiling the child.
- Inappropriate or unrealistic expectations lead to power struggles and cycles of worse and worse behavior.
- Respecting a child's agenda rather than expecting obedience encourages cooperation.
- Fears of future ingrates and deviants fuel expectations that are too high.
- Adjusting unrealistic expectations and empathizing with a child's desires is not backing down or giving up. It is modeling effective behavior.

Practice:

- Get in the habit of asking yourself, *What am I expecting?* in situations where you get resistance. Then ask, *How able is my child to do what I expect given her temperament, age, and stage of development?*

- Even if your expectations are perfectly appropriate, understand that children don't like being told what to do and when to do it. Let your child know what you want done and ask her when you can expect her to do it. Expect that she will need a reminder.

- If your child is consistently not behaving in the way you expect, try adjusting your expectation and focus on what your child *is* doing well, even if she doesn't do it often.

- Sometime when things are going smoothly, ask your child if he ever thinks that you are expecting too much from him or that you expect him to be someone he's not.

CHAPTER 5

The Fifth Principle: Connection Strengthens Relationship

Any obstacle in your child's way of success is your opportunity for connection. Connection happens easily when things are going well—when we're having fun. But what do you do when a problem arises for either you or your child? Forget about it and hope for the best, try to fix it, or connect with your child and strengthen your relationship?

Through connection, we gain direct access to the root of any problem, any obstacle our child may be facing.

When we are connected, we can ask for cooperation when we are having a problem. It is our means of establishing mutually open communication. Connection always bridges the Gap.

The Gap

When communication shuts down and parental influence is blocked, a gap is created. Over time, it broadens and deepens until communication becomes almost impossible between a parent and a teenager. As soon as young children are seen as manipulative, parents begin to distrust and control. Punishments are enforced by the time a child is barely able to walk. Toilet "training" turns into an ongoing battle, toddlers are reprimanded for their impulsive behavior, and daily life becomes a struggle. Every crying episode is seen as a meltdown, and temper tantrums are viewed as manipulative. Children are misunderstood. Is it any wonder they become confused, frustrated, and resistant?

The Gap is the space created between parent and child when the parent's intention is lost in anger, distrust, or fear and the message the child receives is completely different from what the parent intended.

Stress, confusion, fear, and misunderstandings fill the Gap. When gaps are common, children become parent-deaf in self-defense. Authority and positive influence are lost.

Maria thought she had left her boys watching Saturday morning cartoons while she was doing laundry, but as she came up the basement stairs, she heard shrieks coming from the living room. Couch pillows had been thrown around the room, furniture was out of place, a chair was on its side, and the boys were slugging each other with throw pillows. Jason, eight, was on the floor while ten-year-old Matthew straddled him ready to strike.

"What on earth are you doing?" Maria screamed. "Stop it this instant, do you hear me?!" Laughter erupted from the boys. Maria assumed they were laughing at her. "How dare you destroy my living room? Stop all this noise and get to your rooms, now."

Matthew collapsed on the floor saying, "Mom, chill." Incensed and feeling disrespected, Maria grabbed Matthew's arm and pulled him up. "There will be no bike ride this afternoon, do you understand me. Now get to your room until I tell you to come down."

Matthew stomped up the stairs and slammed his door, shouting that his mother was stupid, while Jason slunk out of the room and out of his mother's range. Both boys felt angry and unfairly treated but expressed their feelings quite differently.

Situations like this are common in most households. Nothing horrible, nothing abusive. Control takes over when parents fear their children will never learn to take responsibility, never listen, and behave disrespectfully—forever. When children turn parent-deaf, the screaming gets louder, the threats get emptier, and children learn that they can keep doing whatever they are doing until the parent reaches the latest breaking point. The Gap widens.

Learning to Make Connection

If we want our children to listen to us, we need to say what they can hear.

Not give them what they want, simply acknowledge and respect what they want. Not ask them to solve our problems or take responsibility for our feelings but see both sides. We need to learn how to say what our children will listen to before expecting cooperation and peace.

Connection does not mean hugs and kisses and happiness abound. Connection can occur through conflict. It is a way of communicating that encourages listening and talking and feeling important to someone—interaction. Disconnection occurs when we are indifferent as well as critical, blaming, and punitive. Studies show that children who get in trouble either at home or at school are the ones who feel disconnected. When disconnection happens, more trouble follows. When people feel disconnected from the family, community, or world at large, they have no reason to respect their rules. They have disdain for authority and often engage in misconduct. Connection, on the other hand, is a preventive measure against risky, rebellious, and defiant behaviors.

Who Owns the Problem?

Begin by looking at whose problem it is. From the objectivity of our meeting room, it was understood that the pillow-throwing incident was Maria's problem. So were her assumptions that the boys were being rude and never took her seriously. The boys were having fun. They didn't care that couch pillows were thrown and the room was a mess. Pillows felt better than fists, and they weren't fighting. Their mother's anger seemed unjustified to them.

In order to connect, Maria would first need to own her problem and acknowledge how she felt without making them responsible for her feelings. Instead she dumped her problem on them, and punished them to teach them never to make a problem for her again. In the heat of the moment it's hard to see this, but the boys sensed unfairness and reacted, each in his own way. Maria has just as much right to her anger as her children have to theirs—as long as she owns it. If Maria yells, "What happened?! The living room is a wreck. I can't stand it!" she is owning her problem. Children's radar is strong and senses the unfairness when we make them responsible for our problems. When children don't feel unjustly accused, they are more likely to cooperate with what we need.

The following are examples of expressing feelings but owning the problem:

- "I will not allow anyone to hit me. And you must never allow anyone to hit you. You are very angry with me. Tell me what it is you want to say."
- "I'm having a hard time concentrating. I know you just want to have fun. I need some quiet."
- "I hate feeling ignored. What do you need to be able to hear me?"

See Your Child's Point of View

Step into your children's shoes and listen to what you sound like. Then ask yourself, How would I like hearing what I just said?

Connection requires empathy—being able to see the situation from your child's viewpoint and hear what you sound like to your child. You will never understand completely, but your effort is what keeps you connected and respectful.

Consider Agendas

Maria's kids were having fun. Their agenda was to build forts with furniture and have a pillow fight—maybe even stay out of the way since bike rides had been promised if their parents' chores were completed early. Maria's agenda was to get the laundry done, clean the kitchen, and make her phone calls before bike riding. She requested cooperation. Now the living room was a wreck. Frustrating? Absolutely. Cause for anger and punishment? Probably not—especially if she didn't take on their problem of cleaning up the living room. If she had told them that the room had to be clean and orderly before anyone could go for a bike ride, she would have held them accountable for their behavior—no blame, no reactive defense, and no punishment. But when she saw another big job added to her list, she blew up.

Say What Your Children Can Hear

When we yell a lot of negatives, "Stop it," "Don't," "Why can't you ever…?" "If you do that once more…" the focus is on what's wrong. Children hear blame. Who wants to listen to that? Why do we think we have the right to talk to our children differently than how we expect them to talk to us? The deeper into the Gap you are, the more negative your words sound. The closer to connection you are, the more positive or objective your words—much easier to respond to. A well-intentioned lesson can be interpreted by your child across the Gap as a threat, demand, putdown, or accusation. Through connection, that same lesson can be heard and understood. Phrases like "You never listen," "I'm so disappointed in you," "You are so mean," or "You're going to be the death of me" can lead to serious self-esteem issues on the other side of the Gap.

Using Connective Communication

Connective communication is the most important skill in parenting as it includes so many of the principles set forth here. It is perfectly simple, makes total sense, works, and is one of the hardest skills for most parents to accomplish. Why?

- Because we don't see how important it is to be as respectful of our children as we want them to be of us.
- Because we fear that allowing negative feelings will lead to inappropriate behavior.
- Because we don't understand that the release of emotions is the best prevention of misbehavior.
- And because it doesn't come naturally—we were not spoken to this way.

For most parents, learning connective communication is equivalent to learning a foreign language. It initially feels awkward and wrong. We think it indulges and condones the behavior we don't want. When it is not heartfelt, connective communication can sound patronizing to children, and they reject it. When it is genuine, it can change relationships.

Connective communication is respectful, trusting, empathic, and validating. It lets children know their feelings are normal. It is inquisitive without being interrogating. It allows feelings to vent, and it gets to the root.

The Steps of Connective Communication

When your child has a problem or is behaving inappropriately:

1. *Stop what you are doing and give your child your full attention.* Do not attempt this when your emotions have escalated.

You can always come back to the situation later. Sometimes it is helpful to make eye contact, and sometimes it is better not to.

2. *Disengage.* Stop inappropriate behavior but do not react to, judge, or criticize the behavior. Then put the behavior aside temporarily and go for the root.

3. *Name the problem without criticism or blame,* so your child can hear you.
   - "You boys are having a hard time."
   - "You really wish I would say something different."
   - "I really don't like it when clothes are left all over the floor."
   - "The television needs to be turned off."

4. *Do not try to fix the problem or rescue your child from it.* Take all problems seriously. Never deny or belittle your child's feelings with, "Why are you crying about a thing like that?" Don't start telling your child what she should do or say.

5. *Empathize with your child's emotion.* Validate and reflect back what you hear, see, or guess is going on. Giving words to emotions lets your child know she is normal. Remember: feelings are always okay. Boys are more likely to open up when active—shooting baskets, playing catch.
   - "I totally understand how angry you must have felt."
   - "I wonder if you were feeling left out."
   - "You must have felt really confused by what your teacher asked."
   - "I guess you were really angry at your sister to have hit her."

Don't worry about putting words in your child's mouth. If you are wrong, your child will be happy to tell you so. Mean what you say. If your words don't sound sincere, your child will shut down.

6. *No questions—yet.* Think of a period at the end of your sentence. Without a question, your child is free to listen and doesn't have to answer. Questions put him on the spot and may feel interrogating. You are giving the problem your best guess. Your child will either take it in silently, agree, or disagree. These are good sentence beginnings to keep you from questioning:

- "You must have felt…"
- "I bet if I were you…"
- "I wonder if…"
- "I'm guessing that you must…"
- "I can hear that you…"
- "It sounds to me like…"
- "I know just what you mean."
- "I feel the same way when…"

7. *No buts!* Putting a "but" after your empathizing statement wipes out your intention. "I can understand how angry you must feel, *but* you know you can't hit" tells your child you care more about the hitting than his feelings. He's back to feeling blamed.

8. *Rechannel emotions and energy into acceptable behavior.*
- Give your child pillows to hit, Play-doh or clay to squish, or paper to rip.
- Time him while he runs from the fence to the garage or up and down the stairs. Give her a punching bag or a trampoline.
- Allow one couch, bed, or mattress for jumping on or kicking.

Bonus Points

1. Share a story of your own illustrating that you have felt the same way. "I hate getting up in the morning too. It's my least

favorite part of the day." Or make up a story about another child going through a similar situation. "Once there was a little girl whose mother went away on a trip, and she felt very, very sad."

2. Allow in fantasy what can't be in reality.
   - "If you could say anything you wanted to her, and no one would tell you not to, what would you say?"
   - "Imagine everything in this kitchen was made of ice cream. What flavor would the refrigerator be? Which would you eat first?"
   - "Pretend you could push a button and wings would fly out from your bed. Where would you like it to take you?"
   - "Pretend you had a magic wand and could turn you/me/ your sister into whatever you wanted. What would it be?"

3. For the preverbal child, simply state what happened. It is comforting to a young child who has lost control to hear you put her experience in words and normalize the situation after the crying begins to subside. "You wanted the blue plate, and I gave you the red plate. You had a picture in your mind of your sandwich on the blue plate, and when you couldn't have it that way you felt sad and mad at me for not giving you the blue one."

The Problem with Questions

As we will soon see, questions are very important when you help your child to problem-solve.

But if you want your child to open up and expose the root of the behavior, stay away from questions.

If a parent asks, "Why did you do that?" or "What are you so mad about?" the child feels set up, pressured. He wonders, *Do I answer what Dad wants to hear or what he doesn't want to hear?*

What if his honest answer is, "Because I hate her and wish she were dead." Will he get in trouble? Would his father understand that he doesn't really mean it, he just needs to blow off steam? "I don't know" is his safe exit from the hot seat. But if a parent offers, "I bet you wish your sister wasn't around sometimes," he will feel safer to release angry tension.

Questions often carry blame, so a defensive answer, maybe a lie, is sure to follow. A mother asked her son, who had started lying to her, "Why do you lie to me all the time?" His answer was, "If you don't want me to lie, stop asking me questions." Many children also fear disappointing a parent with a truthful answer. Statements don't require answers. The child doesn't even have to respond. But he can take it in. He may need time to process his thoughts.

Being Your Child's Ally

Perhaps the strongest argument for connective communication is that it helps children make sense of difficult situations. From abuse to death or loss to violent behavior to simple misunderstandings, if the problem is never expressed, it can harm a child's emotional development forever. Your child needs you to be her ally. If not you, she may try to find someone else.

When she knows you will listen and not judge or criticize her, she will trust you and know she can turn to you, no matter what.

Even a child's inexcusable behavior can be talked about and resolved once the feelings that provoked it are acknowledged and validated. Then the problem can be put in proper perspective. Even feelings of terror and abandonment can be normalized so the child can feel balanced again. Learning connective communication gives you the tools to provide this process for your children.

The Child Who Doesn't Talk about It

If your child is an introvert, he is likely to process his feelings internally instead of talking things out, like the extrovert. Don't worry. He's figuring things out before he commits to words. One of the beauties of connective communication is that by using statements to connect, you are not expecting a verbal response. If you can put the situation into validating words, even your introvert can hear the empathy, not feel blamed, and put the pieces together internally. When you give words to possible emotions, you are modeling for your nonverbal or preverbal child, and the connection is still happening.

Being Your Child's Sounding Board

Sometimes we don't need to say much but simply provide a sounding board so our children can get it out, hear themselves, and allow the deeper roots to emerge. Some children are so sensitive to being patronized or are suspicious about what we're after that we need to simply be that sounding board before attempting connective communication. Detaching from the situation enough to avert reaction and allow your child to rant, no matter how annoying it gets, can open doors to those roots. When children are given the opportunity to talk things out to a neutral person, they can often find the direction to take to solve their own problems. Sometimes all they need to do is express their feelings to be done with the problem. It is the rare but artful parent who can detach enough to allow this to happen.

Steps to Becoming a Sounding Board

1. *Detach.* Temporarily ignore the words or behavior. Imagine the behavior sailing over your head rather than slamming into you.

2. *Don't try to fix the problem or teach a lesson.* Remind yourself that your child is having a problem, it's not about you.

3. *Look to the root.* Understand that there is an emotional cause beneath the behavior that needs to emerge.

4. *Listen.* Take your child seriously and listen to what is being said without judgment, criticism, blame, or reaction. Take dramatic words with a grain of salt.

5. *Deflect.* Let the words bounce back to your child so she can hear herself.

6. *Trust.* Encourage your child's ability to solve her own problem. She may need your help, but trust her lead.

One Saturday morning as Eleanor was cleaning, she reminded her three boys to shower, eat breakfast, and get dressed before playing so they would be ready when their friends arrived. As usual, she reminded them three times before anyone seemed to hear her. On the fourth go-around, the oldest and youngest followed her request, but Nick, her middle son at age six, went ballistic. He started screaming at his mother, "You liar, you lie! You never said we had to take showers. You're lying!" Leaving his words alone, Eleanor explained reasonably that she had asked them to take showers, silently wondering if she had left that step out on the one reminder that he actually heard. She said, "Nick, if you want to play, you need to do those things first."

Now in his bedroom, Nick continued his "liar" rant, but suddenly midstream his tone changed and Eleanor heard, "You never play with me, and all you care about is the house being clean, and I don't care about that!" The root had emerged. "You're a liar" was childology for "You're always too busy."

She immediately went to Nick and said, "Oh, so you're upset because you want to play with me, and I'm cleaning." (A statement ending with a period, naming the problem, and validating his feelings.) Nick said simply, "Yes." Eleanor asked Nick what he would like to play, he told her, and she said after he took a shower she would do just that. He quite pleasantly said, "Okay," took his shower, got dressed, and went outside to play with his brothers to wait for his mom. Eleanor made sure she followed through with her promise. Nick felt heard and accepted—the need that was lurking at the root of his behavior was addressed so the behavior disappeared.

Rechanneling Energy

When children have revved up to fifth gear and can't bring themselves back down without intervention, it is important to remember that their energy has overpowered them, not that they are being defiant and disobedient. Because you know this child wants to be successful, is battling an obstacle, and his behavior signals his emotional state, you can intervene with help rather than criticism or punishment.

Rechanneling the energy tells your child that he needs to do something different with his energy, not that he is bad for having it.

In a fit of rage, a child low on impulse control and high on stress can easily turn that energy into hitting or kicking. Objects are thrown, doors are slammed, and parents, siblings, and pets get hurt. Isolating this child in time-out or her room only increases the upset unless you remain with her. But if you are enraged, fuel is added to the fire as she has to react to your energy as well. Staying out of your child's problem and not taking it personally allows you to remain calm and redirect her energy to an appropriate target.

Aside from the usual—punching bags and pillows, clay, drawing—one family invented "Beat-Up Buddies." Each child used an old pair of footy pajamas that they stuffed with pieces of foam rubber. Each was zipped over a stuffed animal or doll to provide a head.

There are as many potential outlets for rechanneling as there are needs for it. When you remain calm, you can remove the overwhelmed child to another room to change the environment. Holding, hugging, and simple touches offer a calming energy. Rechanneling into reading, cuddling, or walking allows the child the time to downshift back to neutral. But they need your calm influence—isolation only increases the problem.

Don't Patronize

When connective communication sounds phony, children feel demeaned. If your child covers her ears or says, "Stop talking like that," that is your cue to take even the tone of a "but" out of your words, get more honest and to the point, or more sophisticated with naming the problem.

Very young and preverbal children love to hear back exactly what happened. "You felt really angry when you got hit. That pencil got pushed right into your arm. See, there's even a mark. It really hurts." Your empathic description of the experience feels like a warm blanket of validation. But once your child gets savvier, his reaction might be, "Duh, Mom." As children get older, we need to get right to the point. "You're obviously angry with me about something. Instead of hitting your sister, tell me what you're mad about" is better than, "You're feeling really angry." And be careful your tone isn't adding, "... *but* you can't hit your sister." There is never an age when connective communication doesn't work.

Don't be afraid to go for the real deal. "After I heard from your teacher what happened today, I wondered if the fight you must have overheard last night between your father and me was upsetting you in school." If that's not the case, you'll likely hear, "What are you talking about?" to which you can reply, "Oh, good. I'm glad that wasn't it." But if it is, you've dug out the root.

We can connect with our children's feelings, agendas, and wishes and still not share their opinions or allow behavior we think is wrong.

"I can understand why you feel that way about your coach" is not saying, "You're right, your coach is a jerk." "You must have been so angry that you couldn't stop yourself from punching your brother" is not condoning the punch.

Putting It All Together

Once you understand the importance of being a sounding board, and are able to use connective communication, you help your child dig into her feelings and get closer to problem solving.

When my daughter Molly was in third grade, she had difficulty with a girl assigned to sit next to her on the bus. Sally was a year older and teased Molly daily. One day I watched Molly coming up the walk from the bus and knew by the look on her face that it had come to a head. She walked in the door, threw down her backpack, and burst into tears. I carried her to the couch and held her while she cried and cried.

"She makes me so mad, I hate her!" Molly finally got out.

I let her know that I understood then dug deeper. "I bet you wish you could punch her." It's in there. No need to keep secret your child's darkest wishes or fantasies. They are often the strongest roots.

"I wish I could pull her arms off," she screamed.

"I bet you do—and her legs too," I said. Then, "I think we need the punching pillow." I brought over our big square pillow used for times like this. She grabbed it from me, threw it on the floor, and began to jump up and down on it yelling and crying. Molly was used to this process and was able to get her feelings out quickly.

"What do you want to happen, Moll?" Once her feelings were out, asking the question got her thinking. It was not my problem to solve, nor was it up to me to tell her what to do about it.

She kept jumping, as she yelled, "I want everybody to get mad at her. I want you to get mad at her, I want her mother to get mad at her, I want the bus driver to get mad at her, I want her teacher to get mad at her. It's not fair! Doesn't she know I have feelings too?"

There it all was, spilled out onto the punching pillow. Instead of telling her that she should ask to have her seat changed or tell Sally how she felt or call the bus driver myself, I asked, "What would you like to do about it?"

Her tears and anger were subsiding. "I want you to write her a letter," she said with amazing determination. I went to find a pad and pencil to take down her dictated words, but at this point, I thought I would burst if I didn't get to the bathroom! I asked her to hold her thought. When I returned, I picked up the pad and pencil and said, "Okay, Moll. What do you want to say to Sally?"

Cuddled comfortably on the couch, she muttered from behind a book, "Not now, I'm reading." My heart sank. Once Molly got absorbed in a book there was no way to coax her back. Frustrated, but plotting to return to it after dinner, I put the pad down and left her alone.

At dinner that night, we began as usual by saying something we were grateful for. My husband, my son, and I went. It came to Molly, who usually passed. As casually as commenting on the weather, she said, "I'm grateful I worked out the problem with Sally." She didn't have to send a letter. She just needed to vent her feelings in a safe, supportive environment and know that she was understood. All I needed to do was let her—first by being a sounding board, then by acknowledging her feelings and fantasies. Molly never mentioned another word about Sally. I can only assume being heard and acknowledged gave her the strength she needed.

When We Think We Know Better

Without connection, we miss the opportunity to understand another's point of view or get another side of the story. We naturally make assumptions, see situations from our own perspective, and draw our own conclusions. We think we know best and children should always listen to us.

A story that came up in a private session shows how easily a parent's conclusions can lead to unfair treatment and unnecessary resentment. Pam has two daughters, Abigail, six, her mother's button-pusher, and Ava, ten, her easygoing child. In our session, Pam said, "I can't figure it out, but I'm suddenly having problems with Ava. I don't know what's going on. She's being quite mean to Abigail, putting her down, teasing her, and just not acting like normal." We talked about a few things Pam could try until a story came out that explained it all.

Their favorite twelve-year-old cousin, Josie, called one evening as the girls were getting ready for bed. Pam called Ava to the phone first and told Abigail that she could talk after Ava was finished. Underestimating Abigail's determination to talk now, Pam let her get on the extension instead of dealing with another meltdown before bed.

By the time Abigail got on the phone, Ava and Josie were chattering and laughing. Although all three girls had a great fondness for each other, Ava and Josie, being closer in age, had more in common, and Abigail was always racing to catch up. Abigail picked up the phone, heard their laughter, and joined them in the only way she knew how—by being silly. Nonsense words and noises amused the older girls for about thirty seconds, but then Ava told her sister to stop. Abigail continued, and Ava's patience wore thin. Soon "Stop it, Abigail" turned to "Shut up, Abby. Get off the phone right now. You're being stupid."

Overhearing only Ava's words and now dealing with Abigail's tears, Pam yelled out to Ava, "Why would you say something like that? You don't have a monopoly on your cousin, you know." All week, Ava had been uncharacteristically taunting and poking fun at Abigail and was beginning to call her names.

I told Pam that I thought Ava was justified in her frustration toward her sister. Her side of the story would be that Abigail barged in with little girl silliness to her "mature" conversation. Of course she would be annoyed and angry. Pam agreed but still couldn't get over Ava's rudeness.

"Be sure you're not asking Ava to compensate for Abby simply because Ava is more compliant," I suggested. "You're setting up sibling resentment that way." Pam realized that's exactly what she had been doing.

Reconnecting

After that, Pam talked to Ava about the phone call. She confessed that she hadn't taken into account how frustrating it must have been for her when her sister suddenly broke in and got silly. Ava told her mother that she did try to get Abby to stop, but she wouldn't. Pam acknowledged Ava's attempts and that she must have reached her limit. Ava's behavior toward her sister returned to normal.

Reconnection can happen hours, days, weeks, even months or years later. It's never too late.

Don't Take It Personally

In order to be a sounding board for our children, we need to be able to deflect their words and behavior.

Not taking it personally requires understanding that your child's problem is not yours to fix—only to help with. It's not about you.

Even words like, "You're a liar" signal that this child is upset. It is your clue that he is off track and out of balance. He needs to get those feelings out in a safe, supportive atmosphere far more than he needs to be told to stop talking like that or be punished for hurting his mother's feelings. Once the feelings are out and emotions are down, the problem can be addressed, as we will explore in Chapter 7.

We take it personally, especially when kicking, biting, hitting, and name-calling are involved. Physical aggression is very common for two to five-year-olds. They often don't know how to handle their sudden intense feelings so they impulsively express them physically. When we assume they are being mean or violent, we are taking it personally. It becomes about us—what they are doing to us, what we have to do about it, how they are inconveniencing us, or what we have done to create such monsters. This is where the exhaustion of parenting comes from—our assumptions and the emotions those assumptions generate. We get ourselves so worked up and worry about where this behavior will lead that we can't be present in the moment to help our child solve his problem.

When very upset, young children are unable to, first, comprehend what is going on with them, second, put words to that, and third, express those words in a reasonable way. But we want reason. We want their anger to go away, and when we can't make that happen, we feel inadequate. So to avoid that, we put them in time-out or send them to their rooms and feel satisfied that we have done our job. Alternatively, we try to cheer them up and rescue them by giving in, buying them something, or getting out the candy—all options that deny their feelings so we can feel better about ourselves.

Handling Tough Dilemmas

Hard times always call for connective communication, but when feelings are overpowering, talking is often avoided altogether. Fears arise that our children will not be able to cope and that their emotions, if given license, will make things worse. So in the name of protection, when we don't have an answer, we don't talk about it.

Betsy came to me soon after there was a suicide in her family. She understandably had some very strong feelings she was dealing with, and five-year-old Lilli had overheard a good deal of crying and wailing from her mother. Lilli knew about the death but couldn't make sense of what had happened to her mother. She suddenly did not want her mother to touch her, put her to bed, or have anything to do with her. I suggested that Betsy address Lilli's feelings and also explain very plainly what was happening to her rather than try to protect her from sadness. An answer was impossible.

"I was lying down with her one night," Betsy related, "and Lilli said, 'I don't want you to put me to bed. I don't like you. I hate your clothes. I don't want your clothes to touch me.' I said to her, 'It sounds like you are feeling upset and frustrated with me because I have been acting differently. I have been upset and haven't been able to be the kind of mommy that I want to be.' Before I had a chance to say more, Lilli said, 'I just want things to go back to normal.' I said that I did too and explained that they would in time, but that when people die, things change, and it's hard for a while. Lilli asked if I would start taking her and picking her up from school again, and if I would be at home at night more. After I answered yes, she asked me to rub her back and cuddle with her. This was the first time she allowed affection from me in over a week." Things slowly returned to normal for Betsy, but that night was a turning point for Lilli. She continued to use her mother for comfort.

In *The Body Never Lies: The Lingering Effects of Hurtful Parenting*, Alice Miller claims that, "Repressed, disassociated emotions can make us ill but not conscious feelings that we can give expression to." No matter how traumatic the circumstance, once the roots can be attended and voice can be given to the emotions in a safe and understanding environment, almost anything can be processed, consciously managed, and even healed.

Main Ideas from Chapter 5:

- Connection creates direct access to a problem or an obstacle by addressing the root.
- The Gap is the space created between parent and child when the message received by the child is entirely different from the message intended.
- Children turn parent-deaf when they don't like what they hear.
- Owning your problem means taking responsibility for it and not blaming it on your child.
- Connective communication acknowledges, validates, and gives release to pent-up feelings that could otherwise fuel misbehavior.
- Connective communication helps the nonverbal or introverted child by not requiring a response.
- Children need allies and sounding boards.
- Empathizing and validating do not condone behavior.
- Connective communication requires detachment—not taking it personally.
- Reconnection can happen at any time. It is never too late to go back over a situation.
- The exhaustion of parenting comes from the emotions generated from automatic and reactive assumptions—from taking it personally.

Practice:

- Become aware of situations where there is a gap between you and your child—an issue you feel unable or uncomfortable to address, a misunderstanding, or something your child doesn't want to talk about.
- Ask yourself how your child perceives you in that situation. What would he say about you if he were describing the situation to someone?
- Think what he would like to hear you say—not giving him what he wants but something validating, connecting.
- Use connective communication if you can detach and remain neutral. Notice how quickly you want to ask questions and get to a solution. Hold an air of genuine curiosity rather than interrogation.

CHAPTER 6

The Sixth Principle: The Behavior I Focus on Grows

We all want to bring out the best in our children. So why do we feel compelled to harp on their worst? Do we really think that will encourage their best to show up? When we punish, blame, judge, and criticize, we focus on their worst, and then expect those accusations to motivate them to be their best. As parents, it is our responsibility to highlight the qualities we want them to develop and draw out the attributes they may not know they possess.

After a child has been yelled at enough, hears that tone of voice enough, feels that anger enough, he will lose faith in himself and develop the qualities we most fear. Our greatest nightmare—what we try so hard to eliminate with punishments and threats—can be exactly what we set in motion. What we focus on is what gets our energy. What we put our energy on grows.

When much of our energy focuses on the negative,
what we get is negative. If we focus on the child
as a problem, that problem increases.

Most parents put negative attention on the aspects they find most irritating or troubling assuming the child will want to change. But if a child hears, "What's wrong with you?" "Why are you so mean?" "You never listen." "You're selfish." "You're lazy," he identifies himself with those attributes.

But when we focus on our child's capabilities and potential, separate from any problem he may have, problems become more easily managed. When we trust in the child's ability to overcome a problem, that is often what happens.

Mindful Focus

Placing focus on qualities and attributes is quite different from praising or rewarding behaviors we want.

Praise and reward depends on the end product being successful.
But mindful focus can encourage even when very little
about the child is successful.

It requires using all the previous principles to see that our child needs help overcoming obstacles, supported by our faith in a positive outcome. Beneath the obstacle lies the child's desire to be successful and often hidden from recognition are the qualities and the potential to reach that goal. If we shine our light on those qualities, especially the ones our child has lost sight of, those qualities will grow.

Dr. Edward Hallowell, child and adult psychiatrist and author of many books, including *Driven to Distraction*, believes that every child is born with talents and passions that can remain hidden if not discovered and encouraged by the important adults in their lives. Especially when criticized, they can be left feeling stupid. They can languish for the rest of their lives never knowing they had talents and passions that could, when nurtured and guided, lead them to fulfilled and happy lives.

In a given day, which of your child's behaviors do you tend to notice or pay attention to? Which behaviors grab your energy? Which ones does your child see you watching the most? Rest assured, those are the behaviors that your child will use when he wants your attention. It doesn't matter to him that the attention is negative. Those are the behaviors that will grow.

A child climbing in a tree is yelled at, "Get down right now, you're going to fall and hurt yourself." The intention is to protect the child from falling. But the parent's fear and anger at the child for climbing the tree sends the child the message that he is not capable of climbing well. The parent highlights the danger he is in. If he listens, he will lose confidence and be more likely to fall. Remember the Gap? Children listen to what they hear, and they hear the message they perceive, not the intention behind what is said. It can actually be a good thing when children turn parent-deaf! If on the other hand the child up the tree is talked down with clear instructions on where to put his feet, the focus is on what he can do and what he is already in the process of doing. He is more likely to get down safely, confidence intact. The child learns an excellent lesson in climbing. Talking about the dangers can wait until he is down and safe.

Children need to be guided through a process, not pressured to reach a result. It's the journey, the learning process—difficult or not—that is important. When we mindfully focus, we see that process and give them energy to blossom and grow on their own terms, not on ours. Rewards and praise are intended to pull our children in our direction—to get them to do what we want. Mindful focus means we see who the child is and encourage a stronger foundation of self-esteem and self-confidence.

Focus on the Positive Within the Problem

If you are worried that your child is afraid to try new things and lacks self-confidence, find the times that she is asserting herself. For instance, if she reacts strongly about something—"Mom, I am not going to try out for basketball. I don't care how much you want me to, I don't want to"—irritating as it may be, try, "Well, you certainly know your mind. No one's going to be pushing you around anytime soon. As much as I don't like the waste of the registration money, I must say, I admire your certainty." By complaining, "Why won't you ever try anything new? You're never going to get anywhere this way," you are undermining the quality you want her to develop. You are setting her up to fail. At that moment, she has no choice but to focus on how incapable she is and what a disappointment she is to you.

If her temperament makes it hard for her to take risks, she is more likely to take a few if she feels understood by a parent who says, "It's hard sometimes to move into new territory. You like to check things out and not rush into anything. That's a good thing. Your impulses will never get the better of you."

If your child seems unable to stand up for himself or assert himself with others, you may fear he will always be bullied. When he is fighting with a sibling try something like, "Boy you got really mad about that. I can see how important that game is to you. You wanted your turn on the computer and you really asserted yourself. Do you think there is a better way of getting your sister to acknowledge what you want?" Or let's say he also gives in to his more demanding sister and you worry he will always take the easy way out. The next time he gives over something she wants (it could be a nurturing temperament and has nothing to do with being intimidated), try, "You are so accommodating to others. It seems like harmony is really important to you. Don't you wish the world was run by more people like that?" Another time you can question whether he feels okay about letting her have what she wants or whether it is a problem for him.

You can turn difficult situations into positive learning experiences depending on your perception of the situation. It will feel awkward at first, but once you understand the principle behind the words, you will see that you are giving your child the support he needs.

Perhaps the root of his inappropriate behavior will be addressed when you focus on the aspect of his character he himself fears he is lacking.

Perhaps your child is way too aggressive for your peace of mind, and you catastrophize that the amount of hitting, shoving, and pushing he does will soon leave him without friends. Catch him being gentle. Instead of being obvious and praising normally expected behavior, "Good for you for being gentle," go for the subtlety he may be more able to hear. "Look at how Pockets rolls over and actually smiles when you stroke her belly so gently like that. See how her lips turn up. That is so cute! That must feel so good to her."

Our children need our encouragement and our belief in them, *especially* when they are showing troubling behavior. When it's hard to find those moments of competence, it's easy to criticize and blame. We amazingly think our negative comments will teach them to shape up. But when the good moments, even when few and far between, are watered and fertilized, competence will grow.

"Islands of Competency"

Dr. Robert Brooks, author of many books, including *Raising a Self-Disciplined Child*, and a faculty member of Harvard Medical School, encourages parents to find a child's "island of competency." In his extensive work on resiliency and encouragement, Dr. Brooks has learned that:

> No matter how far off track a child has gotten, there is at least one small area in which competency can be found and supported.

Like a diamond in the rough, it will sparkle when we shine light on it. It means playing detective, and it requires, for most of us, going against the tide of popular opinion. Punishment is what is traditionally called for when behavior is unmanageable. But punishment is the worst possible antidote. It reinforces the child's belief in his incompetency. We must reach deep inside to find each child's "island" and pull it out so he can see it reflected in our eyes—one of the most difficult things to do in the face of behavior that can make you scream.

First, remember children want to be successful and fear is an obstacle that fuels negative behavior. Perhaps this child feels hopeless compared to more successful peers or siblings, has taken in messages from parents or teachers that he isn't good enough, or has been labeled as the problem in school. The obstacle could be huge.

Second, understand that your child is not his problem or his obstacle. See them separately. His problem—hopelessness, grief, defeat, anger—is the obstacle that has developed in his life for whatever reason. A sense of defeat comes upon a child forced into an environment in which he feels incompetent. That internal state may exhibit as boredom, disdain, disinterest, or disrespect. But those defensive behaviors are rooted in the problem of defeat, not in the child. When the parent can see the child, separate from the problem, he may be able to find himself.

Third, there needs to be a belief in the child's unique competency. Perhaps school does not engage him. It doesn't mean he is not competent. It means that so far school has not caught his interest and he has no motivation to do the work required. Finding his "island of competency"—whether it is horseback riding, skiing, history, computers, dancing—will boost his self-esteem and encourage your hope in his future.

Rewards and Prizes Versus Mindful Focus

We want our children to cooperate with us and be successful at whatever they do. When something does not come easily, motivation is key. Psychologists and human behavior specialists look at two main categories of motivation—*intrinsic* and *extrinsic*. In other words, motivation that comes from within and motivation that comes from outside.

All the behavioral techniques, the rewards and punishments we use to get children to do what we want, are extrinsic—outside manipulations and tactics to make that dangling carrot work. Whether it is the reward of the gold star, the praise of "you make mommy happy," money for good grades, computer privileges, or banishment to one's room, time-out, threats of getting in trouble, or revoking computer privileges, outside motivation techniques only work as long as the external factor is present, that is, the authority figure who holds the carrot or the stick.

Children who are kept in line by the hope of reward or the fear of punishment tend to flounder when the carrot or the stick isn't around.

Then parents think they cannot trust the child to behave appropriately without rewards and punishments to keep him in check. These methods never encourage a child to behave appropriately because it feels right inside. The child never develops intrinsic motivation, because he is too focused on what's going to happen to him or what he's going to get.

Alex's elementary school uses a reward system that gives children "Gotcha" stickers for being kind or responsible without being asked. The sticker shows a big thumbs-up and earns eligibility in a lottery drawing for a prize at the end of each week. At the end of snack time in Alex's class, his teacher asked the children to clean off their desks to be ready to move on to the next activity. Tyler, who had the desk next to Alex, had gone to the bathroom, and Alex decided to clean off his desk for him. When Alex's mother picked him up that afternoon, he was grumpy and combative. After asking him what the problem was, he finally complained, "I cleaned off Tyler's desk without being asked and didn't get a Gotcha." It was clear to Alex's mother that Alex was after the sticker, not the reward of knowing he had helped out his friend. Chances are that Alex either won't bother next time or else will make himself much more obvious.

In order to focus on what she wants to grow, Alex's mother would do well to point out the generosity Alex showed in helping his friend. She must start by validating his disappointment because that is where he is at the moment. Then she could suggest how good Alex must have felt inside knowing he had helped his friend and ask how he would have felt if he had been Tyler returning to find his desk cleaned off. Talking about whether or not Tyler thanked him could generate a conversation about how we feel when our help is ignored or appreciated. These comments might shift Alex's focus off the sticker to his kind deed.

When motivation comes from within, the child associates certain behavior with feeling right inside, achieving a state of emotional balance (success). Intrinsic learning means the child learns for the sake of learning as an end in itself, rather than as a means to an end—a reward.

> *Goals set and earned are intrinsic rewards for the person who sets the intention and accomplishes what he wants. They are motivators to set further intentions. But when the goal is set extrinsically, motivation ends when the reward is either won or lost.*

We assume that once the child matures, the external motivators of rewards and punishments will have trained the child to behave properly. There are two fallacies with this thinking. First, children are not rats in a maze. They have minds of their own and personalities in all shapes and sizes that often resist, test, or fight the authority figure when they feel trapped, coerced, or manipulated. And second, research has shown that extrinsic learning goes no farther than what is perceived necessary to achieve the reward. In his book *Unconditional Parenting: Moving from Rewards and Punishments to Love and Reason,* Alfie Kohn sites studies that show, "…extrinsic motivation is likely to erode intrinsic motivation…The more that people are rewarded for doing something, the more likely they are to lose interest in whatever they had to do to get the reward."

No reward in the world can give a child a desire to cooperate and help others, a love of learning, a passion for whatever moves her. How many reward systems have actually dampened a child's potential because she never pushed herself past the reward of the gold star or the A? How many children who achieve an A with no effort work twice as hard because they love learning? How many children who know there is a pizza waiting for the reader of the most books or pages are going to choose *Huckleberry Finn* over lots of short easy reads? If computer privileges are systematically removed for bad behavior, then the child is going to hoard her computer time, fearing that at any minute it could be taken away.

External motivation can actually foster complacency, laziness, boredom, and lack of cooperation or interest, Kohn says. The external motivator loses its value after awhile and the child will up the ante if he is used to being rewarded for normally expected behavior. "Sure I'll take the trash out if you give me a dollar."

Wendy confided in me that her eleven-year-old son, Christopher, said to her that it was clear he "wasn't wanted in this family." Instead of rolling her eyes or saying, "That's ridiculous," Wendy looked at Christopher seriously. "Every time Dad walks in a room he gives me a direction or orders me to do something. Half the time you do it too. I even lost swimming privileges for not hanging up my towel, which was an accident. There are consequences for even the most trivial, accidental things."

Wendy realized that she and her husband had been overly focused on what Christopher was doing wrong without even realizing it. They were missing him. And things were starting to go downhill with their six-year-old, Patrick, as well. We talked about shifting focus to the roots Christopher had so eloquently exposed. The patterns of yelling and punishment needed to change for both boys. Two weeks later, Wendy told me, "Already the thinking has changed in our home. Both my husband and I are trying to deal with what's going on underneath the behavior rather than just the behavior—it really helps. We've had a couple of real shining moments and more clarity than we've had in a long while." She shared this story.

Their year-old puppy had been a serious behavioral problem and a target for jealousy between the boys. Her potentially dangerous biting behavior had meant that Patrick was not allowed to pick her up, so Christopher was more involved in the training process. One evening while Chris was doing some training with the dog, Patrick deliberately lured her away with food. Chris yelled at Patrick, and things escalated until Patrick got hit and started screaming. Normally Wendy would have yelled at them and sent them both to their rooms. This time she changed her focus.

"I abandoned dinner preparations and tried to focus on their feelings. Suddenly it became perfectly clear to me. I said, 'Patrick, you must be feeling jealous that Chris gets to do more with Rosie than you do. He can pick her up and cuddle her on his lap, and he gets to do most of her training.' Well, Patrick said 'Yes' in a way that broke my heart. And I could see the light bulb go off in Chris' head. His whole body, voice, everything changed. We all got it! Then I told Patrick how I had noticed that Rosie was getting more comfortable with him because he had been so gentle with her. And I reminded them about how much Rosie's behavior had changed in a year thanks to Christopher's impressive training. Two birds with one stone! From then on they have worked out a way for Patrick to be Rosie's 'aide' while Chris continues his training. The best thing is that Rosie is loving it!"

Gold Stars and Other Unintended Punishments

Sticker charts can be used to stop a habit the child wants to break. When it is in black and white, or shiny colors, the child can see that he is indeed capable of changing the behavior he is motivated to change, for example, a four-year-old who desperately wants to wake up in a dry bed, a seven-year-old who wants to stop pulling her hair out, a ten-year-old who wants to see that she actually is accomplishing goals at piano. They don't work for long when the stickers are given for behavior the parent wants to see. Prizes at the end of a "good" week lose their charm after awhile.

Children whose parents give out check marks and smiley faces to induce behavior they want typically feel angry, frustrated, or hopeless when they get a check minus or a frowny face.

Rewards are dependent on approved behavior, on a product accomplished. So no reward is like a punishment. In classrooms, it's always the same children who get the rewards. The ones who never do get consistent negative reinforcement that they are not as good and give up trying early on. And awards given to every child in a class or on a team soon become meaningless when children see through the attempts at dishing out self-esteem.

Praise Is Overrated

Self-esteem was the parenting buzzword of the eighties. High self-esteem is a wonderful goal, but it becomes undermined when we misunderstand how to accomplish it. When we praise to the hilt thinking we are increasing our children's self-esteem, it backfires. We are now experiencing an epidemic of entitled twenty-somethings many of whom require so much praise in the workplace that companies are hiring praise consultants. Like rewards, praise can undermine initiative. Conversely:

Praise feels condescending to a child when it accompanies something the child does not feel proud of.

And many children become suspicious of praise when it feels manipulative.

A father came to see me concerned about his son's lack of self-esteem. He explained that his son was mad about a paper he had written for school and threw it on the table saying, "It sucks." His father picked it up, quickly looked it over, and said, "What's wrong with it? I think it's great." His son stormed upstairs and slammed his door. I suggested that his son was not suffering from low self-esteem but frustration at a father who "doesn't have a clue," as his son put it, I added that he would have been more helpful to his son if he had acknowledged his feelings instead of denying his point of view. "I guess this didn't come out the way you'd hoped. Can you tell me what it is you don't like since I don't see it?" A creative parent could put mindful focus on what he would like to see grow in this child with, "You have such high standards for yourself that it's hard for you to let anything slide by. That is going to serve you well in your work. Although it makes you pretty hard on yourself."

When praise is useful, it is specific and descriptive. Instead of "good job" or "you're such a good girl," pay attention to what it is you like. "I really appreciate it when you bring your dish to the sink," "It was kind of you to offer your sister a push on the swing." But stay away from praising normally expected behavior like, "Good for you for coming when I called you," or you will have a child who expects praise for everything. "Aren't I a good boy? I just had a poop."

The Problem with Blame

Whenever we place blame, we leave our children with no other option than to be defensive.

"But he hit me first...She made me do it...You never let me do anything I want."

Blame is like a blanket condemnation, and for that moment anyway there is nothing left to grow that is positive. Laying blame is like watering shame and self-deprecation. "I'm stupid...I can't do anything right...I should just kill myself" are phrases parents hear from children who feel blamed. "You're stupid...He's such a jerk...She's lying" come from children who are deflecting blame and projecting it elsewhere. There is no opportunity for the blamed to take in what happened before hiding behind a wall of defense. The child has to blame back, deny his actions, possibly with a lie, justify his actions with anything he can come up with, or suck it up and retaliate later on the one he perceived got him in trouble. Blame does not hold anyone accountable. It merely creates feelings of fear and anger. Even the child's name called with *that tone* feels like blame. Imagine living in your child's head. Can you guess how much of the time she is afraid of getting in trouble or blamed for something? And of course, the more she is blamed, the more trouble she gets in, because the blame only expands the obstacle in her way of successful behavior.

Life Inside the Box

It's not always easy to find those "islands of competence" or unique qualities to admire, especially when the negative behavior is all you can see. Parenting a strong-willed child can get oppressive when there seems to be no letup to the demands. You feel boxed in. Clarity and objectivity are a dim memory. When emotions are high and solutions feel out of reach, your child's point of view is the last thing you care about. Within that tight space, your assumptions seem like the Truth with a capital *T*.

Carol's three-and-a-half-year-old does not like to stay in her car seat. Sadie will often unhook her seat belt and climb into the way-back with her brother. The last time this happened, Carol stopped the car and went around to her daughter who was balancing on the back of the seat. Carol yelled, "You get back in this seat and buckle your belt. Why do you keep doing this?" As Sadie was climbing back, she yelled, "I don't want to sit here." Carol pointed her finger very near Sadie's face and said, "You will sit in this seat because I told you to." Then Sadie slapped her mother's face.

Carol saw red. She was not about to look for any roots. She grabbed Sadie's little arm and squeezed it. Her face was not pretty. She needed to get away from Sadie so she could think.

Time is important. Take all the time you need.

I asked Carol what she ultimately wanted for Sadie. She said, "For her to do what I tell her. And not to feel like she won't listen to me." Carol's priority is off. She is stuck in her box with her own agenda. Outside the box, she would objectively be able to see that she wanted Sadie to be safe and to take responsibility for herself by staying buckled up—a more worthwhile goal than getting her to obey. Outside the box, Carol can focus on what she wants to grow by appealing to Sadie's sense of logic and pride.

I suggested that Carol find a time when both she and Sadie are in a good place and not during or just after a car ride or a slap in the face! Carol would then raise the issue of the unpleasant times they have had in the car. In order to connect, she would need to start by acknowledging that being strapped in a car seat is no fun for Sadie who wishes she could be in the back with her brother. By acknowledging Sadie's agenda first, Carol can more realistically expect her to listen. Sadie is at the height of egocentricity. If Carol tells her what to do and expects her to do it, she will tune out or resist. Hence the slap—inappropriate behavior but understandable given the fun she was having, her persistent temperament, and egocentric stage of development together with the angry, blaming finger coming at her. The slap was Carol's signal that Sadie felt little, powerless, angry, and misunderstood.

Appealing to Your Child's Sense of Logic

This is where the art of parenting comes in. After connection has been made, Carol can nurture Sadie's better qualities with, "I'm not sure you're old enough, but I do know you're smart enough to understand why it's important for you to be in the car seat. Do you think you're up for learning about it?" This little challenge will likely appeal to Sadie as three-year-olds are hungry for information about how things work and why. I suggested that Carol demonstrate with a toy car and toy people what happens when the toy car hits something hard. Then instead of telling her, ask Sadie what she thinks happened to the people.

"Do you think they might be hurt? How? What do they need to do now? Who can help them best?" Involving Sadie in the drama will help her better understand how the car seat protects her. Telling a toddler that she has to stay strapped in or she could get hurt makes little sense.

Handing Over Responsibility

Now the magic step: Giving Sadie responsibility for herself by focusing on her capabilities.

When we tell children what to do, when, and how to do it, the message we send is, You have to do what I say, because you don't know any better.

Even if that is true, children like Sadie don't like to hear it. Sadie's desire is not to be defiant. She did not slap her mother because she has no respect for her. She slapped her because she was so mad at being coerced and having a finger pointed in her face that her impulses took over. She is perfectly willing and able to cooperate when she is treated with the respect she is demanding—the same respect Carol wants. Just because she's little doesn't mean she doesn't need respect.

Carol can then say to Sadie, "You have a responsibility to take care of your body and keep it healthy and safe. It is your body; not mine, not daddy's, not your brother's. Sometimes in order for us to take care of ourselves we have to do things we don't like. I have to wear a seat belt too. And sitting in a car seat is one way you can do that. I will always be there to remind you when you forget, because it's my job to make sure you're safe. If you forget, I will stop the car and say, 'Remember to take care of your body Sadie.' Can we agree on that?"

Carol would then be putting her priorities in order, focusing mindfully on just what she wants to grow in Sadie and teaching her a very important lesson—all in a way that will encourage Sadie to rise to the challenge.

Main Ideas from Chapter 6:

- Focus on negative behavior promotes negative behavior. Focus on capabilities, even potential capabilities, promotes them.
- Mindful focus is unlike praise or rewards. It can build positive capabilities even in the midst of negative behavior.
- Your child has at least one "island of competence."
- To influence your child's behavior, focus on and trust the child's unique competency rather than wrongdoing.
- Motivators are either intrinsic or extrinsic. Extrinsic rewards motivate no further than the win or loss of the reward. Intrinsic rewards keep motivating.
- Rewards become punishments to the child who doesn't get them.
- Praise is overrated and can undermine a child's initiative. Feeling appreciated builds initiative.
- Normally expected behavior should not be praised.
- Blame and accusation build walls of defense. Defensive behavior is the only option.
- Telling children what to do puts focus on their inability. Asking them what could be done builds competence.

Practice:

- The next time your child does something inappropriate, jot down a few notes about what happened to remind yourself of the incident. When you have time, think about what positive character aspect of your child was evident. Even if her behavior was inappropriate, what about the energy behind the behavior could you focus on and validate (for example, her determination, strong mind, knowledge of what she wants, sticking up for herself or a friend)? When emotions are cool, reconnect with her and let her know that even though you didn't like her behavior, you saw an aspect of her character that you admire. Then ask her how she could use that quality with a different choice of behavior.

- Make a list of your child's "islands of competence." Perhaps it's longer than you think. Then find times to point out specifics to your child that he might not think are true of him, such as, "I noticed how carefully you carried that Lego unit you built. You didn't drop one piece."

- List aspects of your child that you have concerns about, such as, lack of enthusiasm, aggressiveness toward others. Then look for times when you see the opposite and can point out what you want to grow. "You seemed so energized about that phone call. It must have been something that got your juices going." "You really put your energy behind your words more than your hands today with your brother. Words can be very powerful, can't they?"

CHAPTER 7

The Seventh Principle:
Problem Solving, Not Punishment,
Teaches Responsibility

M om, you have to find out what to do instead of sending me to my room when I do something wrong,
because it doesn't work, you know. All it does is make
me mad." This five-year-old boy sent his mother to her parenting
class with this assignment. Remember when you were a child
and were sent to your room or grounded? Did you use that time
to think about your actions and contemplate a better way? I
doubt it.

When I sent Molly to her room and she climbed out her window, slid down to the porch, and ran off, I learned that she would
not tolerate what she considered unfair treatment. I had a choice. I
could come down harder and harder with the strong possibility of
raising an insurgent, or I could find out what to do instead. I learned
that when I treated her with respect and logic, she responded in
kind. Punitive reactions to misbehavior do nothing to teach responsibility—unless out of fear. As I learned, and have witnessed with so
many families, they actually promote future misbehavior.

Children hate to be punished, and the parents I know hate to punish. They just don't know what else to do. Punishment has been with
us for so long, it's hard to trust that fairness and logic will teach anything—a foreign concept when it comes to disciplining children.

With punishment, children either "behave"
out of fear or "behave badly" out of defense.

115

When children who have been punished do behave, they do so because their temperaments are adaptable and their motivation is to please, not because of the punishment. Adaptable children are the easiest to mold to our wishes. They are also the easiest to motivate with fairness and logic. However, they respond obediently to punishment and usually do not fight back when treated disrespectfully. So we believe that punishment works. But children who take punishment with no argument are likely to repress feelings of unfairness and resentment.

If trouble is not showing up in misbehavior, look for physical signs of stress or tension, for instance, frequent stomachaches or headaches, hair pulling, stuttering, bed wetting, withholding bowel movements.

Control Versus Authority

"How can I maintain control of my child if I don't punish?" This question is based in the fear of losing control. The pressure is tremendous. This parent may be looking for a replacement for punishment but wants the same result. Some form of coercion is all that can be imagined. This parent cannot trust a balanced relationship where mutual respect promotes cooperation, where discipline affects the internal motivation of children so external methods of control become obsolete, where mistakes are opportunities for learning, and where non-directive parenting allows for children to be problem-solvers.

Being in control of yourself, having personal power and confidence is what grants authority.

True authority means the ability to gain the respect of and to influence or guide another. It has nothing to do with controlling another and all to do with controlling yourself. Positive influence does not happen when you are holding power over your child.

The Problem with Punishment

When children are afraid of getting in trouble, they may do as they are told to avoid the trouble. A few problems with that:

- In order for a fear tactic to work, what the child fears must be formidable.
- Parents have to be ready to follow through with the fear tactic and maintain consistency with it.
- Many children resist fear tactics.
- Those who don't may behave to avoid what they fear but will not learn the intrinsic value of right and wrong. They just learn not to get caught.
- The relationship with the child is risked when the child fears the parent.
- A relationship based on control through punishment is fuel for rebellion.

Think of the last time you felt humiliated or put down for not doing what someone wanted you to do. Did that humiliation encourage your cooperation or stimulate your anger and resentment? If you did what they wanted, why did you? Did you feel coerced, trapped, misunderstood, unfairly accused? Chances are this is how your child feels when she is punished.

Punishment can cause children to be vengeful, sneaky, rebellious, and retaliatory, often taking out their feelings of humiliation and shame on siblings, peers, or pets.

Bullies are children who feel powerless at home and find their power elsewhere. Malevolent parental authority in childhood leads to disrespectful, irresponsible behavior in teens who desire to retaliate against authority. Clearly, punishment does not lead to responsible behavior. If responsible behavior develops from someone who was punished, it is likely that respect, love, and communication trumped the punishment—in which case the punishment was not necessary.

The Meaning of Discipline

We automatically associate discipline with punishment. We need a new definition for discipline. The best I found is "the ability to behave in a controlled and calm way even in a difficult or stressful situation." I would call this the self-discipline of a confident parent—the best modeling for a child's own self-discipline.

Structure, yes. Limits, absolutely. Rules, of course. We all need limits to successfully live in society among others who have rights the same as ours. Limits are for the purpose of maintaining mutual respect. In the family, every member deserves to feel respected. On the road, every driver deserves to feel safe; therefore, every driver must respect and behave according to certain rules of the road. Every driver knows ahead of time that if the rules are broken there are specific consequences. But if a driver is arrested for illegal parking, it becomes a punishment that is unexpected and unjust.

The same must hold true in a family.

Children should know the consequences for behavior ahead of time. When rules are clear, children know what is expected of them and what they can expect in return.

This is the definition of good discipline. Rules need to make logical sense to the child in order for them to be internalized.

When internalized, they will be upheld even in the absence of the authority figure.

When a punishment is either arbitrarily given at the time of misbehavior or is illogical to the misbehavior, the child does not expect it and is left feeling angry and resentful. He usually has no right to contest. He must accept the injustice. Over time, he learns the system is unfair but eventually expects arbitrary rules learning in the process that he must deserve his treatment. He grows to adulthood, fears or distrusts authority, and passes his fears on to his children. He doesn't know any other way.

Look for the Fear Beneath the Anger

Children's aggressive, even violent behavior is usually an expression of anger. We think if we can stop the anger the behavior will disappear. So we punish anger. We rarely recognize that anger is a self-protective defense against fear.

Fear always is the root of anger and violence. To curtail behavior resulting from fear, we must address the fear.

We increase fear with threats, angry voices, and punishments. How can increased fear motivate "good" behavior?

If behavior is the result of combined internal and external stimuli, negative behavior is the response to fear-inducing stimuli. Each person experiences fear differently. For some children, defiant behavior at bedtime can be provoked by the fear of going to sleep and perhaps having a nightmare. Changing from one activity or place to another can trigger fear in a child who has a difficult time with transitions. The fear provoked at the thought of speaking to an adult or joining in with other children can freeze an introverted child. Even boredom can be the cover for fear of not doing well enough or meeting certain expectations.

The Power of Choice and Consequences

Children need to experience the consequences of their behavior. But when we fix their problems, sometimes by punishing, they don't learn the natural consequences of their own mistakes.

We are too attached to being right to trust our children to solve their own problems.

We nag endlessly, we get into power struggles to make them see it our way, we force coats on, and make special meals so they don't learn the consequence of being cold or hungry. We don't want to deal with meltdowns so we give in, and they don't learn delayed gratification. We can't stand them to be sad or unhappy, certainly not angry, so they don't learn how to handle their emotions. And when they misbehave, all we do is dole out a consequence—the politically correct word for punishment—withholding computer or television privileges, grounding, being put in time-out. These are not consequences. They are punishments. But we feel better when we call them consequences.

The simplest means of giving consequences is by posing a choice and handing over responsibility for that choice.

"Do you want to lower your voices or play outside?"

"Do you want to put your coat on or take it with you?"

"Would you rather hand me that truck or shall I take it?"

"Do want to turn off the TV or shall I?"

"You can either do your assignment or get a bad grade; it's up to you."

When children have the opportunity to make choices, they feel strong. If they refuse to make the choice, you can offer to make it for them. The power of the choice, when offered genuinely, is one a trusting child will rarely turn down.

A three-year-old whined about not being able to get her shoes on. Instead of criticizing her with, "Stop whining," her father said, "Do you want to put them on yourself, or do you want me to do it?" She sat back sniffling, held her feet out to her father, and stopped whining. The same child picked out the dress she wanted to wear the night before. As is appropriate for her age, she often changed her mind. When she wanted her good dress, her mother said, "Not a church dress, but you can choose this one or that one." Sometimes there was frustration and whining, but she always made the choice.

Her older brothers were fighting with each other because one had lost the coins that had come with their pirate ship. After arguing about who did what, their mother said, "I will give you a choice. Either forget about them and be thrilled when they show up, or you both go and look for them now. Which do you choose? If you can't, I will make the choice." They chose to look for the coins, stopped fighting, and found them a few minutes later.

There's Always a Choice
When Molly was five, she needed glasses. She had to wear a patch on her eye, have drops in her eyes, and listen to her eye doctor call her "honey." One day she refused to go to her appointment. I somehow got her in the car, but when we arrived, she didn't want to get out. She said, "I haven't decided yet whether I'm going in or not." As I reached in for her hand, I said, "You don't have a choice about whether or not you go in, but you do have a choice about how you feel about it." This intrigued her. She took my hand. I continued with, "You can be really angry about this, not like your doctor, and hate your glasses. Or you can tell yourself that your eyes are part of your body, and you are taking care of your body with glasses that help your eyes. Your eyes are yours for the rest of your life, and you will need them to be in the best shape they can be."

We walked on quietly. I ventured, "So have you decided which you will choose?" She said very thoughtfully, "Not yet." When we reached the door, she said, "I guess I'll be okay about it."

She hopped up in the doctor's chair like a trooper. She never complained again about her glasses and took excellent care of them for years. She had been handed a choice that helped her feel important and understood. She took it instead of being the victim of circumstances.

What to Do Instead: The Shift to Problem Solving

Connection is the most effective way to address the fear and stress that provokes inappropriate behavior. Chapter 5 gave you connective communication tools to address the roots of the behavior. Often it is enough to give vent to the feelings for the behavior to disappear. But when it isn't enough, when we need to guide children to choose different behavior, the final stage of connective communication is problem solving. This is where we shift from statements to questions. This is what holds children accountable and teaches responsible thinking and decision making.

Punishment is easy—and makes kids mad. Problem solving is hard—but has logic and fairness imbedded in the process.

Problem solving needs to be learned, and takes time—but far less time than the arguing and power struggles that result from threats and punishment.

Camilla was four, had quite a temper and had taken to throwing things. Her mother, Melanie, shared a simple story with me. Camilla was angry about being told she had to put her toys away. She picked up a plastic strawberry and threw it under the table. Angrily, Melanie told her to pick it up. Camilla did, only to throw it again—at Melanie. Melanie picked up the strawberry and put it in her pocket. Camilla fell to the floor in a fit of rage, screaming that she hated her mother. Melanie, rougher than she liked, took her to her room. The screaming continued for quite some time. Camilla learned nothing from this incident.

A strong-willed child—any child for that matter—would respond better to logic and a challenge. After the second throw, Melanie pick up the strawberry and say, "You are very angry with me about putting your toys away. You have a choice to make. You can either put this strawberry in the bin where it belongs, or I will put it in my pocket. Which do you choose?" A tantrum may occur anyway if Camilla's stress level is too high to manage. After the tantrum has subsided is a good time for problem solving. "You were mad at me, and you threw that strawberry because you were mad. What do you think is the best thing to do with the strawberry now that you got your mad out?" Most likely Camilla will now put the strawberry where it belongs. Then Melanie could offer, "Would you like me to help you put the rest of your toys away or can you do it yourself?"

Engaging the Child in the Problem

Problem solving involves asking some form of the following questions:

"How can you make that happen?"

"How can we make this work for both of us?"

"What would you like to do about it?"

While our traditional definition of discipline leads most parents to think in terms of control, punishment, and obedience, problem solving encourages us to think in terms of guiding, thinking, and negotiating.

Instead of judge and director, telling the child what to think, do, and say, the parent becomes facilitator and guide of the child's thought process by asking questions and gently leading him to accountability and decision making. But the outcome may not be what the parent expected.

Telling children what to do and how to do it teaches very little. "You shouldn't feel that way. He's your best friend. You need to say you're sorry. You've hurt his feelings, and he's telling you he doesn't like it." All well intentioned, but the child either parrots or ignores the direction taking no responsibility for his problem. And the parent's way of handling the problem is not necessarily the best way for the child to handle it. Children are usually way more creative than we are and have a language of their own. Instead, try problem solving. Notice how it is interlaced with connective communication:

> **Parent:** "You look pretty upset right now. Something must have happened."
>
> **Child:** "Sam sat with our 'enemies' at lunch today and wouldn't let me sit with them." (His answer will be "Nothing" if he thinks you will tell him what to do.)
>
> **Parent:** "Oh, wow. That must have felt crummy coming from your best friend."
>
> **Child:** "He acted so stuck-up. What's with him, anyway?"
>
> **Parent:** "Have any idea what might have led to it?"
>
> **Child:** "No. He's a jerk."
>
> **Parent:** "Maybe you need a little time away from each other?" (a question, not a direction)
>
> **Child:** "I don't know, maybe. I did get really mad at him in math class today."
>
> **Parent:** "Oh, really. What was that about?" (not critical, genuine curiosity)

Child: "He butted in with the answer. He thinks he's so darn smart and has to let everybody know."

Parent: "Sounds like you took offense and let him know."

Child: "Yeah, so now he's snubbing me."

Parent: "What do you think you'd like to do about it?"

Child: "I don't know. I don't feel like talking to him."

Parent: "What do you think might happen if you don't talk to him?"

Child: "He'll probably think I hate him and snub me even more."

Parent: "Do you hate him?"

Child: "No, I just get mad when he thinks he's so smart. I'm smarter than him, but I don't show it off."

Parent: "Do you think you can let it go?"

Child: "I guess, it's not really that big a deal. It's just that we both agreed we didn't like those kids he sat with today."

Parent: "So you feel kind of betrayed."

Child: "Yeah."

Parent: "So what do you feel like doing about that?"

Child: "I want to tell him that he's a suck-up."

Parent: "How do you think he'd respond to that?"

Child: "He'd call me some stupid name, probably."

Parent: "How did his sucking up make you feel?"

Child: "Mad—and left out."

Parent: "What if you told him that?"

Child: "I guess. He'd probably say he was sorry. I guess he was really mad at me for saying what I did."

Parent: "I know you will know the right thing to do when the time is right."

This parent skillfully guided her son through his own thoughts to help him come to his own conclusion. Her son was able to think it through and name his feelings because this kind of process had been happening for a while. He trusted his mother. She wasn't attached to the outcome. She trusted he would work it out in his own way.

This may sound like an episode of *The Brady Bunch*, and many children find it hard to engage for so long, but when we get in the habit of guiding conversation like this, children are forthcoming because they trust our neutrality, and they want to work it out. When we tell them what we want them to do (what we would do if we were in their shoes), they tune out and lose their ability to problem-solve. A typical answer to "What do you think you should do?" becomes a very lifeless "I don't know."

This type of conversation takes awhile to master. Your child needs to trust that you do not have ulterior motives that may suddenly appear. The key is remaining neutral and knowing it is not your problem to fix. You don't have to have the answer. In fact, you shouldn't have the answer. It is so much easier than you think.

Accountability and Logic

When your child has made a bad choice, he needs to be held accountable. Contrary to popular opinion, punishment does not teach accountability. Problem solving does. The child is again engaged in the solution, and will follow through when it seems fair and logical.

Jeff, age eight, is a morning dawdler. School was several miles away and driving him herself was not an option Michelle could always afford. One morning, Jeff missed the bus. Assuming his mother would take him, he started playing basketball in the driveway. Watching him through the window gave Michelle a minute to collect her thoughts. She told him to stop playing basketball and come inside. Then she said, "I have to be at a meeting at 9:30 almost an hour away. Missing the bus has put me in a terrible crunch, and I need your help. I need you to feed Lucy (the dog) and take out the recyclables."

Jeff tried, "Okay, but how about if I feed Lucy, and you take the recyclables out. It will save time."

Michelle countered, "No, because I have to make my breakfast and eat." It made logical sense, so Jeff complied. After those things had been done, Michelle said, "Now I need you to get the rug samples from the bedroom and bring them to the car along with the folder on the counter and the movies in the living room that need to go back."

Jeff did what was asked and started playing basketball again.

Michelle called to him, "Jeff, I need you to stop playing and come back inside." He did. "Get a pencil and paper and write a list for me." Michelle dictated her grocery list as she gathered her things together and then asked Jeff to carry her uneaten breakfast to the car.

Once in the car, she asked calmly, "Jeff, do you see how the choices we make affect other people?" (notice she used "we" thereby eliminating blame).

"Yeah."

"What could you do differently so this doesn't happen again?"

"I could use my alarm clock to get up earlier and have more time for resting in the morning."

Michelle nodded and asked, "And what will motivate you to get to the bus on time?"

"If I miss the bus, I don't get to talk with other kids, and on the days I have gym and art, I don't have time before class. The bus gets me there earlier."

Jeff was cooperative with his mother, because he knew he was responsible for causing a problem for her, and he didn't feel accused so didn't need to react defensively—it seemed logical and fair to him. There are still mornings when his slowness causes a problem, but instead of taking away computer time, something that always resulted in battles, Michelle now uses logic.

Logical Consequences

Appealing to the child's natural sense of logic works. Many children have a heightened sense of justice and react badly to punishments because they don't seem fair. For instance, many children have to be held down in time-out chairs or they won't stay. Whatever the purpose of the time-out is certainly defeated. Taking the time to find out what your child responds to saves so much time in the long run.

If a child breaks or harms something, she must buy a new one using her allowance, earning the money, or being involved in the repair. If she leaves her bike out in the rain, she must dry it and work the rust off with products she must buy, or she doesn't get to ride her bike for a while. If she drops food or makes a mess, she is handed a broom and dustpan or cleaning products to clean it up. If her father's tools are left out after she has used them, she must stop whatever she is doing to put them away. Logic works. It rarely gets an argument.

There are plenty of problems that don't have logical answers. If the behavior is the result of heightened anger, it is better to hold the child accountable *after* the emotion has cooled. For instance, calling someone a bad name may require the child to go back and say what he really meant. If a toy is grabbed away and thrown, it must be retrieved and handed back. But if feelings are high, resistance is likely. Cooperation comes more easily after the emotion has calmed.

The best consequence is a choice: Either you do what I ask or experience the consequence, which is set ahead of time with the child.

When Joe asked his parents for an iPod, their biggest concern was that he would be plugged in around the house and in the car so conversation would stop. His parents had some stipulations.

"If we are going to buy this iPod, we would like you to agree that when you are hanging around the kitchen or in the car with us, you will not use it."

Joe asked, "What about if I'm just going to the kitchen to get something and leaving again?" They agreed that would be all right. Other agreements were made about times of the day it could not be used.

Then Joe's dad said, "What do you think the consequence should be if any of these agreements are broken?"

"They won't be Dad, don't worry," Joe said offhandedly.

"But just in case, I think you need to know what will happen," his dad said.

"I don't know. Take it away I guess," Joe offered.

"That makes logical sense," his dad said. "How about taking it away for a day to see if that is motivation enough to remind you." They agreed.

A consequence set ahead of time can offset arguments or power struggles, especially when it is in writing. Then the agreement needs only to be mentioned or pointed to. It is clear. The iPod will be handed over, regretfully, but understandably if, in fact, Jeff is required to do so. It is logical.

Consequences need to be carried out to be effective. Many parents drop the ball at this point because they don't want to upset their child or deal with an argument. "Alright, just this once." Children learn the consequence is not real and pay no attention. Power struggles break out and children are blamed for being irresponsible.

Effective limit setting begins with setting limits on ourselves.

Remember the definition of discipline: "the ability to behave in a controlled and calm way even in a difficult or stressful situation." That is the parent's responsibility. It is not the responsibility of the child to be the grownup first.

Negotiating

Children are masters at arguing and negotiating. This is a great skill to promote.

Children who are allowed to argue their case at home and negotiate decisions think more creatively and often do better in school.

However, negotiating can become endless and exhausting if you don't know where to end it. Your child will not stop first. So negotiate and argue—yes. But when you have come to your final decision, be clear that it is over. Your child may be mad about the decision. That is his right. Your right is to be done. When you engage in endless arguing, you lose authority. You must be the first to disengage. Mean what you say, and say what you mean. Just make sure that what you say is fair and respectful.

How to Negotiate Effectively

- Acknowledge that what your child is arguing about is important to her.
- Ask to hear her side of the story/point of view. Take it seriously.

- State what is important to you/your concerns/your side of the story.
- Ask: "How can we make this work for both of us?" or "How can you make that happen?"
- Be open-minded and willing to compromise, but be clear when you have reached your final answer.

When your child builds a good case with information that supports his claim, and you listen and allow him a win, he builds confidence in himself. A good argument means creative thinking and problem solving—excellent skills for later in life that need to be nurtured. When somebody else always knows better and doesn't take the time to listen, he feels defeated. Allow your child a win when the argument is a good one rather than reacting with an automatic answer. But if you know you will not change your position, let your child know that and stop engaging.

Contracts

When contracts are needed, negotiating takes another step. Usually contracts are written when parents want to change some behavior like television viewing or computer time, but they can be used for a variety of situations. Kristy's boys Trevor, nine, and William, six, loved writing contracts. One contract involved the family choosing specific words to stop another when his anger was elevating. Trevor chose "fart" for the word anyone could use with him; William's was "fire," and the word the boys chose to say when their mom's anger was intensifying was "pudding."

One afternoon Kristy heard Trevor's angry voice upstairs yelling, "Get out of my stuff or I'm going to kill you!" Kristy went upstairs to see what was going on. William was backed far away from Trevor and was cowering. Kristy said, "William what's the word?" Remembering, William stood tall and said, "fart, fart, fart!" Trevor couldn't help a quick smile. It was enough to back down a bit. Kristy said, "William, what do you want to say to

Trevor?" William came closer and said, "Trevor, it makes me scared when you yell at me like that."

The following are some of the contracts that Trevor wrote after talking them through with his mother and brother:

■ THE THROWING CONTRACT

"We the Denby's will not throw things, except for Frisbees, balls, and dog toys. The consequences for the person that throws will be that they will have to pick up the mess and be nice to the person you threw at, and if something broke they would pay for repairs."

■ THE BROTHERS CONTRACT

"We the brothers promise to be kind. Trevor would like William not to touch these certain things: My gun and suction darts, no going in my room without permission, my journal, my new movies. If William asks, Trevor may agree to share these items. William would like Trevor to: share on play dates, no busting in William's room to take film props, not change the TV channel without asking, and not say he hates William."

■ THE BASEMENT OR KID TOWN RULES

1. *No one goes in without permission (from a kid).*

2. *No food without permission (from adult).*

3. *No kids allowed on the gym equipment unless you are over five years old.*

4. *No stealing.*

5. *No punching or kicking.*

6. *No adults without kids permission unless emergency.*

Thank you. You have two warnings; if all the warnings are broken you will go to kid town jail."

■ THE TV CONTRACT

We the Denby Kids will try to remember not to argue about the shows we watch. If we can't agree on a program Trevor will go to the other room to watch his program. We agree to watch only one hour of TV a day unless mom and dad agree to a special movie. The kids do not have to all watch the same hour, but if you choose to, you don't get another hour. No one will walk into the room and change the channel someone else is watching without first asking. William can watch anything on PBS, Nick JR, or another preapproved program. Trevor can watch Nick, Boomerang, Animal Planet, or Discovery channels. For sure there will be no Rugrats, Spongebob, Fairly Oddparents, or Cartoon Network.

133

Here's one a bit more formal written by the parent for her seven-year-old son:

■ COMPUTER CONTRACT

1. *No computer in the mornings before school or breakfast.*

2. *Computer hours are from 5:00–6:00 and 7:30–8:30 P.M. Simon agrees to do homework after school before getting on the computer.*

3. *Simon agrees to get off the computer when it is mealtime.*

4. *The computer goes off at 8:30 P.M. every night. Mom will give one thirty-minute warning and one fifteen-minute warning.*

5. *If Simon fails to address his personal needs while on the computer, the consequence will be loss of the computer for one day.*

6. *If Simon does not follow these rules, the consequence will be loss of the computer for two days.*

We all agree to this contract and to follow the rules stated above.

(Signatures of Dad, Mom, and Simon)

Contracts allow children to have a say, negotiate rules and consequences, and hear other points of view. They foster respect for the rights and needs of others. But most importantly, they empower the contract writers. They can be simple and short, but if they are thought out and co-written—not dictated by the parent—they are very effective.

Empowering Children with Nondirected Play

All day long children are told what to do and how to do it. They are given little opportunity to take responsibility for themselves. If we could look down from above, we would see little pawns being moved around by giants on life's game board. We giants expect that in the moving we are teaching our pawns the right moves so they will do the same when they are giants. But our children are different players, at a different time, and need to learn to play by their own rules.

Remember sandlot baseball, when neighborhood kids would get together anytime they could at the empty lot, out in the street, or at the playground to choose teams and play ball? No coaches, no parents, no supervision. The basic rules of the game provided a structure within which kids decided the rules of playing together and the consequences of not following those rules. Now adults set the rules, the teams, the schedules, the pressure, and the consequences. And it doesn't stop with baseball. How much time do your children spend in nondirected, unsupervised play?

Play fosters imagination, creativity, brain circuitry, and even responsibility. When children are continually supervised and directed, they lose the ability to be spontaneous, to create, and to develop and respect the rules of play and of life. Our attempts to protect our children from harm and to supervise and schedule their lives so we have more control are inadvertently setting them up to fail.

By dictating rules to our children, fixing their problems, and hovering over everything they do, we take away their opportunities to learn by trial and error. Of course, intervention is often necessary, but problem solving involves them doing the thinking and taking responsibility. As we restrain our compulsion to tell them what to do, we risk them making mistakes, falling, and maybe even failing. But if we understand that falling is part of the game, we will also see them gaining the strength to get back up again with a better understanding of how the game is played. A father in one of my workshops wrote at the end, "I don't need to stop her from falling. I only need to warn her about the fall and be there once she has fallen."

The Steps of Problem Solving:

1. Take all situations seriously.
2. Hear your child's side of the story.
3. Listen, validate feelings, and acknowledge the importance of the situation.
   - "That sounds really important to you."
4. Facilitate your child's thinking.
   - "How do you think you could get her to do what you want?"
   - "How much time do you think is reasonable for you to spend playing video games?"
   - "How do you think she feels when you say/do something like that?"
   - "Why do you think he doesn't want to give that to you?"
5. State your concerns. Own them.
   - "Here's what I'm concerned about."
   - "I know you don't care about this, but I do."
   - "Here's what I think…Can we come to an agreement?"
6. Ask your child what he needs. Sometimes just venting is enough.
   - "How do you want this to turn out?"
   - "What do you think you can do about it?"
   - "What do you need from me?"

7. Ask if your child would like your opinion, help, or advice.
8. Ask for what you need. No blame.
   - "I need to feel assured that you will be safe."
   - "I need about an hour of help from you."
9. Allow the child to think it through, guiding with questions rather than directing.
10. Make lists of ideas and cross off any that cannot be agreed on.
11. Make an agreement.
    - "How can we make this work for both of us?"

Each of these steps may take a while and require discussion. Your child may not be happy about the outcome. That's okay. The important step is that you come to an agreement. If you can't, table the discussion and come back to it later.

Main Ideas from Chapter 7:

- Parents who use punishment for control are in fear of losing control.
- Punishment causes children to feel powerless and often leads to sneaky, vengeful, or retaliatory behavior.
- Good discipline requires mutually established rules.
- Fear lies beneath anger. Punishments increase fear, provoking more anger.
- Consequences should be natural or logical, understood, and agreed on ahead of time.
- A consequence should be set up as a choice. "Either this or that. You choose."
- Problem solving is the final stage of connective communication and shifts from statements to questions.
- With problem solving, the parent becomes guide and facilitator of the child's thought process by asking leading questions.

- Negotiating is an important skill—but not to be engaged in endlessly.
- Allowing a child some wins builds confidence.
- Contracts must be co-written so children have a say, negotiate rules and consequences, and honor other points of view.
- Constant adult supervision robs children of decision-making skills.

Practice:

- Catch yourself telling your child what to do or say. Stop, step back, and remember to let your child think for herself. Ask questions to help her make decisions. Remember, you are facilitating or guiding her thought process.
- Watch children's unsupervised play. See what you can learn about their natural ability to problem-solve.
- Practice problem solving again and again and again.

CHAPTER 8

The Eighth Principle: Good Boundaries Mean Good Balance

You are not responsible for your child's happiness is a common refrain that parents in my groups often hear me say. At first, they look at me like I've lost my mind. "Nor are you responsible for your child's feelings or even behavior for that matter." Now they really think I'm loony. "But you are 100 percent responsible for everything you say and do." The light starts to dawn.

"But how am I not responsible for my child? That's what being a parent is," the argument goes. Of course, we're responsible for our children's care—to nurture them, provide for them, and raise them to be good citizens. But taking responsibility for their feelings means that their unhappiness, anger, jealousy, and sadness is our fault and therefore our job to fix. To make them happy is an impossible task, but most mothers I know will go to extremes to ensure that happiness—often sacrificing their own in the process.

Good boundaries underlie the successful application of all the previous seven principles. Boundaries between parent and child are necessary in order for children to learn responsibility, be accountable for their actions, solve their own problems, make mistakes, and learn from those mistakes to have strong intrinsic values. We must be able to let go, stop fixing, rescuing, and taking responsibility for everything they do and say.

"I hate Brian. He's a stupid jerk, and I never want to see him again," says Brian's six-year-old neighbor Will.

"We do not talk like that about our friends. You know you don't mean that." The *if you can't say something nice, don't say anything at all* philosophy is well intentioned to prevent mean-heartedness in Will. The problem is Will's parent is denying Will's feelings and sending the message across the Gap that he is bad for having them. Connective communication, described in Chapter 5, teaches us to first acknowledge and empathize with Will's feelings—"Wow, you sound really angry with Brian"—using more acceptable language and then putting on your detective hat to dig to the root—"Sounds like Brian must have done something that got you feeling so angry." The first response, telling him he can't talk like that, shuts the door on communication; the second opens it. When we shut the door, teaching is far less likely. But the second is not possible if this parent feels responsible for her son's feelings and fears he will become a hateful person, in other words, if she has a poor boundary.

We cannot control our children's feelings. When we do, we come up short in lose/lose power struggles. It is exhausting. As much as we hope for happy children, we cannot make that happen. We can, however, control ourselves and what we do for our children by providing opportunities, modeling appropriate behavior and relationships, and accepting and loving them. For all of that, we are fully responsible. Their happiness, or sense of balance and success, is a product of that.

"My children were embarking on their futures in fragile vessels, and I trembled. I wanted to remove obstacles, smooth their way, I wanted to change their childhoods. I needed to be right all the time, I wanted them to listen to me, learn from my mistakes, and save themselves a lot of grief. Well, now I know I can control my tongue, my temper, and my appetites, but that's it...I can't make good things happen. I can't keep anybody safe...
What a relief."

—*A Three Dog Life,* by Abigail Thomas

Defining a Boundary

A boundary is a protective, invisible shield that separates two people. We know how uncomfortable it feels when someone stands too close. The separation that a boundary provides keeps us each on either side of an imaginary line, not only physically but emotionally. When I have a good boundary between myself and my child, I know what I am responsible for and do not ask my child to take that responsibility for me, and I know what my child is responsible for and do not take that responsibility for him.

The boundary is not a wall that keeps my child out, nor does it prevent me from emotional involvement with my child. It is more of a filmy, permeable drape that wafts in the breeze and never creates a hard and fast line.

With a good boundary, I can be of far better help to my child when he has a problem, because I am not taking responsibility for it. And my child is more cooperative with my problems when he doesn't feel blamed or responsible for them.

It's not always easy to tell where the boundary line is. If my child is expressing anger toward me with, "You're stupid" or "You're so mean," it's difficult to see this as my child's problem. If I yell at her that she can't talk to me like that and send her to her room, I am trying to fix her problem. I must stop her behavior, so I engage in control tactics. But I only fuel her anger toward me. If I can remain detached and see that she is having a problem, I can allow her to work through her problem on her side of the boundary. When she has no more fuel from me to add to her flame, when I don't take it personally (not easy to do), she can work it out—she may storm out, slamming a door on her way. When emotions are calm, I can tell her my problem: "I don't like being called stupid." If I do not feel responsible for her happiness, I can hold her accountable by asking her to say what she meant in a way that won't offend me.

When a parent recognizes and holds a boundary—can let go—a huge weight is lifted. Parenting becomes easier and more satisfying. I can help someone with a problem when it is not my responsibility to fix it. When I make it my responsibility, it becomes about me—I have to have the answer—and less about the person with the problem. I may even blame the one with the problem if I let it become my problem. "How dare you call her stupid?"

If I take on your problem, and feel it is my duty to solve it, empathy is not available to me. I am stuck in sympathy, which isn't helpful. Sympathy may tell you I feel sorry for you, but then I'm in the sorrow with you. I may even add to your problem!

THE DIFFERENCE BETWEEN EMPATHY AND SYMPATHY

Imagine a huge hole in the ground with man A stuck at the bottom unable to escape. Man B comes along and hears man A in the hole calling for help. In his sympathy, man B jumps in the hole with man A. Now they are both stuck in the hole. Man C comes along and hears A and B calling for help. Able to empathize, Man C understands what is needed and says, "I'll be right back." Man C returns with a ladder and lowers it into the hole for A and B.

My mother was a professional worrier. Whenever I had a problem, she worried about it. Then I had both my problem and her worry. I didn't want her problem as well, so there was a lot I didn't tell her. I don't want my children hiding problems from me for fear that I will become a problem for them.

Whose Problem Is It?

We began discussing this issue in Chapter 5. Let's clarify it further. Whoever *initially* has the issue or the upset is the owner of the problem. A messy room is the parent's problem. A child's anger at a friend is the child's problem. Often the line is not so clear. If my child is tantruming in the supermarket, my child has the problem. But when it upsets me and causes me embarrassment, I make it my problem. Then I'm upset about my problem and can't effectively help my child with hers. However, I have a right to stop my child from calling me stupid, and I need to remove the tantrumer. But *how* I handle each issue has to do with my understanding of whose problem it is.

If my child hasn't done the dishes, it's my problem since I'm the one who is annoyed, but I make it his problem when I yell at him for being inconsiderate and lazy. If my children are disruptive at the dinner table, it is my problem—they don't care about table manners—but I make it theirs when I blame them for being ill-mannered. I need to hold my child accountable for forgetting the dishes, and I have a lesson to teach about table manners, but how I go about it—whether I take responsibility for my problem or ask my child to solve my problem—will determine the amount of cooperation I will receive and the lesson I will teach. Children have fine-tuned radar and sense even before we do when we are asking them to take responsibility for something that is our problem. It feels unfair and illogical to them, and they will resist—until it happens enough and they give up learning that they are responsible for us.

If my child hasn't done her homework, it's her problem, but I take it on when I nag and yell and hover until she has it done correctly. She then learns that she doesn't have to take responsibility for it—she knows I will. When my children fight with each other, it's their problem, but it becomes mine when I think I have to solve it.

When it is the child's problem, the parent:	When it is the parent's problem, the parent:
1. Listens as the child initiates communication—even if that communication is behavior only.	1. Initiates communication starting with "I" and without blame.
2. Respects and validates feelings.	2. Acknowledges ownership of the problem.
3. Acts as a sounding board and reflects back what is heard without judgment or advice.	3. Asks for help with the problem.
4. Problem-solves with the child.	4. Holds appropriate expectations and motivates cooperation.
5. Offers help or suggestions but does not fix the problem or rescue the child from hurt feelings or disappointment.	5. Negotiates, makes compromises.
	6. Or owns the problem and does nothing, realizing the child is not responsible.

When children are made to feel responsible for their parents' problems ("How dare you talk to me that way. You make me so mad."), they learn to build a defense to deflect that responsibility and blame. As a result, many often blame everyone or everything else but themselves for their own problems and responsibilities. Or they take on the blame their parents dump on them and feel responsible for everyone.

Lee took responsibility for everyone. She learned to be a fixer at a young age. She tried to make her parents happy so she could relax. Boundaries were difficult with her nine-year-old, Sasha, who was in her first year of public school since home schooling. It was a hard transition. Sasha was made fun of and called names because she was tall and quite strong for a girl. Lee had also been bullied in school but did not want to make a problem for her parents so never mentioned it. She longed for parents who would protect her. She was determined that she and her husband would be the parents she had wished for—parents who charge into school, confront the principal or teacher, and demand their child's rights. She didn't realize that the parents she wished for were not necessarily the parents Sasha needed. What Sasha needed was the self-confidence to stand tall in the face of ridicule. This does not develop with a fixer for a parent.

Initially Sasha felt relieved when her parents said they would talk to her teacher, but the next morning she told her mother not to. Lee went anyway. When Sasha found out, she blew up at her mother. Lee could not imagine that her help was not wanted. What Sasha needed was what Lee had the hardest time giving her—trust in her own capability.

When I asked Lee if she trusted Sasha's ability to face this problem, Lee confessed that she didn't. She admitted that she often told Sasha what to say or do in problem situations. Sasha would come back with, "That's fine for you, Mom, you're strong, but I can't do that." Indeed, the more Lee told Sasha what to say or do, the more Sasha got the message that she couldn't do it right and backed off. Because Lee had learned to rely on herself when she was young to protect her parents from worry or unhappiness, she had developed an arsenal of defense tactics; tactics that Sasha didn't need. Sasha had to find her own.

You Don't Have to Have the Answer

I see parents' shoulders drop in relief when I tell them they don't, actually shouldn't, have all the answers. Lee's answers only underscored Sasha's feelings of incompetence. By not coming up with the solution, only your support and trust, you give your child the opportunity to be successful to find her own way rather than cause interference by interjecting your opinion about her problem.

Can you allow your child to fail at something if that is the best way for him to learn? Can you hold back even if you know the answer to a problem just so he can come up with his own? We so often tell our children what to do or how to do it because it's simply easier. We don't have time to problem-solve. But what do our children learn about competence and ability when we do everything? It's easier in the short run, but in the long run resentment and frustration build when they come to you again and again because they don't know what to do, they're bored, they expect you to do it for them, or they blame you for their problems. You can hardly blame them when you have taught exactly that.

Linda came to me at her wit's end over her ten-year-old daughter, Ashley, who seemed to be controlling the household with her emotional outbursts. Linda was a self-proclaimed controller who had very strong ideas about how things should be. She saw Ashley's behavior as disrespectful, defiant, and rude. Linda and her husband, Jim, found themselves flip-flopping back and forth from reacting punitively to giving in for fear of the next outburst.

As Linda quickly learned, the benefits of detaching from Ashley's demands and refusing to become engaged in never-ending arguments allowed Linda to step out of the power struggles. She got it that she wasn't responsible for Ashley's outbursts. When she was able to disengage, she could actually feel compassion for Ashley's frustration. Success came one day for the first time in six months.

Ashley had come home from school very excited about an invitation to a friend's birthday party. Linda said with a tight stomach, "Oh, that's the weekend of your swim meet, but we don't know yet which day and time you'll be swimming." The next day, Linda called for the schedule. Ashley would be swimming at the very time the party was scheduled. She thought of not telling Ashley. She wanted an answer, a solution, before she picked up her daughter. Then Linda reminded herself that she wasn't responsible for Ashley's feelings, she didn't have to have an answer, and if Ashley had a tantrum, she didn't have to take it personally.

Suddenly able to let go, Linda gave her daughter the news with heartfelt empathy. She waited for the outpouring of anger and blame. Ashley was quiet until they got home. She slammed the car door, stomped up to her room, came back down to announce that she would be eating dinner in her room, and slammed her bedroom door. Her father, Jim, had been preparing dinner and yelled upstairs that she would indeed be eating at the table with them, to which he got a "No, I'm not" followed by another slam. Linda quickly filled him in. Not wanting her daughter to call the shots on where she would be eating dinner yet understanding her distress, Linda called up gently. "We'd really like you to eat at the table with us, Ashley." Ashley opened her door and said, "Mom, if I sit at the table, I'll just get mad at you, and I don't want to do that." Linda was floored. Ashley was taking responsibility for her own anger.

Linda said, "Well in that case, why don't you come down and fix a tray to take to your room." As Ashley was fixing her tray, Linda said, "Thank you for telling me that, Ashley. Also I want to make sure you understand this is a one-time deal." Ashley nodded and went back upstairs. The next day she told her friend that she would have to miss the birthday party. It was over.

"Come on Ashley, it's only a birthday party. We all have disappointments. You're too old for this" would have been the denial scenario. But Linda found a boundary. She didn't try to make her daughter happy, or worse, make her feel wrong for being disappointed and angry. And Ashley didn't have to justify or defend her anger, escalating it to do so. She could handle it alone.

You're Not Responsible for Your Child's Feelings

When children know that their happiness is our goal, they learn to manipulate us to get what they want. When they get it, we teach them that they are entitled to have whatever they want.

When they find that life doesn't dish out happiness, they may look for substitutes in food, sex, drugs, or alcohol—whatever it takes to fill the void.

Sadness, jealousy, anger, revenge, disgust, and hate are all taboo expressions for the child whose parent takes responsibility for her happiness. When parents only want to see positive emotion, because negative would reflect badly on them, children are robbed of the full range of human emotion and may experience shame when they inevitably arise. The child will try to suppress those "bad" feelings, which can lead to more unhappiness and often depression—unless she chooses to use her feelings to thwart her parent. By not freely expressing her feelings and having them understood, the child never learns how to manage them. Sometimes she denies them, keeping them in her dark corners to fester and cause shame, and sometimes they erupt in physical or verbal violence toward others. She then handles those feelings inappropriately when her own child expresses them. Patterns continue when boundaries are fuzzy.

In *Dark Nights of the Soul*, Thomas Moore writes, "Genuine catharsis [to regain a sense of balance] requires the emotions of shame, dread, fear, puzzlement, and even hopelessness. Anything less is too superficial. The avoidance of these feelings, which beg for attention, makes people numb and foggy and therefore incapable of necessary empathy." The full spectrum of feelings is the human experience. We need to embrace our feelings in order to have tolerance and compassion for ourselves and others. Balance requires vulnerability—a willingness to experience all feelings, positive and negative. It's what we do with them that requires self-control.

Don't Expect Appreciation and Gratitude

"But what about how I feel when I go out of my way to do something for him, and he doesn't even thank me? He's completely ungrateful!"

Your resentment is your responsibility, your problem. What you do for your child, what opportunities you provide, is your choice. Many parents compensate by giving their children what they themselves missed out on not realizing the price tag of appreciation placed on every toy, car ride, playdate, and soccer practice. Keep in mind your child does not have your past experience to compare his life to. Why should he be grateful to you for having the only life he knows?

Your child is not responsible for your need to be appreciated.

If I think I'm being a great dad because I'm giving my son the attention I never got from my father, I will expect the gratitude that I thought I would have felt. Not only am I projecting my own unmet needs and setting misguided expectations on my son, but I may even be giving him more attention than he wants. I am going to feel taken for granted and resentful when he ignores me or tells me to get off his back. I provoke his anger or guilt when I storm out, demand his gratitude, or give him the silent treatment. The goal of making him happy got drowned out somewhere along the way.

The irony is that the less we require appreciation for what we do, the more we get it as our children get older. They are free to give it when there are no strings attached. Teach them appreciation for others, and it will come back to you one day. Make sure your children express thanks to others and always write thank-you notes. "Please" and "thank you" around the house need to come from everyone. Model appreciation for others as well as for your children. Like respect, appreciation is learned when it is experienced.

The Value of No and Limit Setting

Parenting young children requires sacrifice and putting personal desires on hold to create and nurture a growing family. But when a parent continually surrenders her needs and desires, she subordinates herself to her child and will inevitably develop resentment when he starts demanding that she do what he wants. "I won't, and you can't make me," may be the voice of a testing toddler, but it could be the child who has come to expect what he wants when he wants it.

Children do not feel safe without limits. When a child holds the power and the family walks on tiptoe, it may look like she is getting what she wants. She is not. She doesn't get to be a child when she has too much power. She wants, as well as needs, her parent to be in control.

You have experienced, I'm sure, losing it and then leaving the room to get away from your child. What happens? She comes after you. She clings, she pounds on the door you have closed, she will not leave you alone. This is not because she is being a brat, it's because she needs reassurance that you are in control of yourself. She won't leave you until you are. She doesn't feel safe otherwise.

Children cannot take power away from a parent without the power being handed over. Saying no to a child, putting limits on behavior, is not only necessary but essential for creating healthy boundaries. Often a no is required to let your child know that a demand is infringing on your rights or someone else's. The desire can be acknowledged, understood, and validated but still unfulfilled. We have a right to say, "I can't do that right now. After dinner I will have more time." Or, "I have to say no to another after-school activity, because I don't want to do any more driving."

A good boundary allows your child the right
to his anger or disappointment without you
rescuing him from his feelings.

Our feelings and desires, our time and plans, our agendas are just as important as our child's. We have as much right to our feelings as our children have to theirs, as long as we own them and do not force our children to take responsibility for them.

And children must have the right to say no to us as well. How else will they learn to say no to a powerful peer if they have never been allowed to say no to a powerful parent.

Saying No Without Saying No

No can be said without actually saying the word "no." The best way to say no, especially to a strong-willed and determined child, is to say, "We can do that, just not right now. Let's find a time and put it on the calendar." Or, "How can you do that without me this time?" Or "Why don't you get it all set up, and we can do it after dinner." Children feel defeated when they hear no enough times, but their arguments and anger are usually not as strong with something like, "Absolutely, you can get a Playstation—when you can pay for it! Do you want to start saving up now?"

Keep in mind that if you begin your sentence with no, that is likely to be the only word your child really hears. *No* is often interpreted as *never* to a young child, so to come around the back door and say what can be done instead is a good way of making it work for both of you. You can avoid the word no yet still set a limit.

Can Parents Be Friends?

I hear again and again from the "experts" that parents should not be their children's friends. Implied is that being a friend is inappropriate and undermines authority, and you cannot set limits and hold children accountable if you are their friend.

Why not? Don't you hold your friends accountable for what they do and say? Good friendships are lost over less. When we can't say no to our friends or be honest with them, it signals a poor boundary. When we know what to expect from our friends and are consistent with what they can expect from us, we have established that line beyond which we do not cross. I see no reason why we cannot be friends with our children.

But in the parent-child relationship, we are much more than friends. We are their teachers, their guides in life, and we are responsible for making sure they are held accountable. This does not preclude being a friend as well.

Raising kids you love to live with embraces friendship as well as responsibility that goes beyond friendship. The problem comes when you are only their friend.

The Power of Modeling

It all begins with how we treat ourselves. When it comes to the day's agenda, where do your needs fall on your list of priorities? Do you spend your time doing for others and never for yourself? Do you schlep your children around, fix their problems, get their things together because they refuse, and give in if a meltdown looms? If so, what is this teaching them about you? What about self-respect—the foundation of respect for others? How would you feel if you said no to your child because you didn't want to add another thing to your plate? If the answer is guilty, then you are teaching your children that they are more important than you. Do you get angry with them for *making* you mad or tired or sick? If so, you are teaching them to be responsible for your feelings. Do you get hit a lot? If so, you haven't taught them that you do not deserve to be hit.

"I can't stand it anymore," is the phrase I heard over and over from a perfectly competent parent. Her third child pushed her over the edge. Drained of energy, even normal, age-appropriate behavior from her three-year-old pushed Jennifer's buttons. Her youngest was needier, clingier, and more aggressive. The more she reacted to him with yelling and blaming, the more demanding and aggressive he became. She was embarrassed in front of friends and relatives who rolled their eyes at his flamboyant behavior, and she felt helpless to control him effectively.

Jennifer had to learn that she was important too. She had put all her efforts into making him change, which, of course, was exhausting and impossible. It took awhile getting there, but once she understood the principle it was immediate. "I always thought if I did it right, he would change," she reported to our class, "but it isn't about him changing, it's about me letting go of what he's doing *to me*." She had drawn her boundary. "He doesn't drive me crazy anymore. And the best thing is, he's relaxing a bit too."

Modeling goes a long way. Your self-worth determines how your children treat you.

If you disrespect yourself by putting your needs at the bottom, why should your children respect you any more than you respect yourself?

Letting Go of the Outcome

If you don't have a healthy boundary, you will take personally everything your children say and do. It becomes your job to right their wrongs, to take away their pain, and to mold them in your image. These are impossible tasks. They make parenting exhausting. The freedom that comes when we don't take their behavior personally, when we don't have to rescue them from unpleasant feelings and tough situations, when we aren't attached to how it all turns out, allows us to be in the moment, connecting, supporting, accepting, and helping.

Letting go of the outcome is the hardest lesson any of us have in life. We can't alter the future but we sure do try. We spend more time worrying about the future and reacting to the past than we do in the present moment with our child. Our practice is to let go.

Power Shared: Finding the Balance

In general, parents fall toward one end of the parenting continuum or the other.

Parents who say yes too much   Parents who say no too much

(permissive) _____ (autocratic)

Mostly we fluctuate back and forth according to our agendas, stress, and patience level. But if we get our buttons pushed, we react automatically and typically end up at one end time after time. Our natural tendencies surface, and conscious choice disappears. We revert to old patterns from our past. Parents who have a hard time saying no (permissive) and parents who have a hard time saying yes (autocratic) create an imbalance of power, have poor boundaries, and hold expectations that set children up for failure.

While parents are the authority figures of the family and are always in charge of how the family operates, power must be shared with the child instead of held or given away so the child learns how to make wise and responsible decisions. This does not mean family authority is shared, but all members of the family must be respected as authorities over themselves. When the child's own personal power is acknowledged and allowed, yet she is not given more than she can handle, balance is maintained, and she feels successful. Giving her limited choices, allowing her to make reasonable, age-appropriate decisions, hearing her side of the story, setting appropriate expectations, and acknowledging her feelings are all ways of supporting her personal power and authority.

The center of the continuum is where we find equanimity and balance—where consistency of responses and expectations see us through the tough times when we are impatient and tired, when the car breaks down, or when crisis hits.

Consistency does not mean doing the same thing in every situation. It means tapping into that inner reservoir of values and principles—your core philosophy of parenting that remains constant no matter what.

When everything you say and do in your parenting generates from that consistent philosophy, your children know what to expect—both of you and themselves. That consistency allows them to thrive, each in their own way, each at their own time. They will cooperate and respect others—at least some of the time. And they are a joy to live with—most of the time.

When your old habits and automatic reactions sneak in, and trust me, they will—often not quietly—they become wake-up calls rather than normal occurrences. It is not without failures and mistakes that we decide what we stand for. We must experience failure to know what we don't want (remember that for your children, too). Your expectations of yourself should be set for success. These principles do not ensure the answers. Don't forget, you don't have to have the answers. In fact, the conscious parent will always have doubt. If you are rarely in doubt, you are parenting on automatic pilot. You will always be walking that fence, coming down on one side or the other. The principles in this book will keep you in touch with the fence so your reactions won't land you in someone else's yard.

Main Ideas from Chapter 8:

- Good boundaries mean I am not responsible for my child's problems, and he is not responsible for mine.
- Taking responsibility for a child's problems means robbing him of the opportunity to build his own capacity to solve them.
- Taking responsibility for a child's feelings means robbing her of her own.
- Sometimes children need to fail so they can find their own answers.
- Children learn to manipulate parents who want their children's happiness above all.
- Entitled children can be products of either tight discipline or conflict-avoidant parents.
- Modeling strong self-worth teaches children they deserve it too.
- Setting limits is necessary for children to feel safe and cared for.
- No can be effectively said without saying no.
- A balance of personal power within the family encourages cooperation.

Practice: Sharing Power

- The next time you get enraged at your child, ask yourself if you were demanding that your child take responsibility for your emotions or behavior.
- Are you a fixer? Do you try to solve your child's problems so he won't have any? Or are you a controller? Do you ask your child to solve your problems? How?

- Pick a day when you will be with your child/ren quite a bit. Draw a line with power kept at one end and power given away at the other. Each time you interact, ask yourself: Am I keeping the power, handing it over to my child, or sharing it in a way that we both get our needs met? Make a dot on the line for each interaction. How did you fare in terms of allowing your child some personal power—but not too much? How many dots come close to the center of the line?

PART 2

APPLYING THE
EIGHT PRINCIPLES
TO DAILY LIFE

CHAPTER 9

The Morning Rush

Morning battles are frequent in the Petrocelli household. At eleven, Finn is still pokey and unorganized in the morning. Being on time is a concept that escapes him. His eight-year-old brother Jake is a little easier to get going, but he gets stuck in whatever grabs his attention. Four-year-old Natalie is in daycare. She never wants to get going and is clingy with her mother, Melissa, who is not a morning person herself. Ken wants his wife to be happy and comes down hard on the kids when he thinks they are making her mad. Mornings are always rushed, and both parents are left feeling guilty and ineffectual as they head off to work—late again.

How Is the Behavior Intended for Success?

Morning power struggles, daily resistance to getting out the door, yelling, being ignored, and being late kept Ken and Melissa in a state of morning frenzy, unable to see anything but stubbornness, defiance, and uncooperativeness in their three children. What they missed seeing was that Finn's pokiness and disorganization were aspects of his temperament inflated by the reactions from his parents. The message to him was *You are not okay the way you are.* Jake was not being defiant as much as distracted. His intense focus on whatever attracted his attention helped him escape from what he didn't like hearing from his parents. Natalie is at the age where the initial separation from parents and home feels like loss regardless of how much she likes her daycare. They were each trying to make things work, but the critical demands on them to move faster and faster made cooperation difficult.

Fearing they hated school but had no choice, Ken and Melissa were afraid of risking chaos if they let up on their threats and constant prodding. But once they examined their morning situation, Ken and Melissa found that the struggle wasn't about school. The boys even said they wanted to be on time to avoid walking into the classroom late and alone.

What Is the Behavior Signaling?

Finn hated being rushed. The more pressure he felt, the slower he moved. Jake would turn parent-deaf when the yelling began and hide himself in a book or game—anything to turn invisible. Natalie refused to get dressed, dug in her heels, and screamed, "You're not the boss of me!" Each had a problem. No one was happy. They were too busy defending themselves against their obstacle to have a pleasant morning—the negative attack strategy of their parents to hurry them. They didn't have a chance to be successful. The fact that weekends were relaxed could have clued Ken and Melissa, but they only saw school and their children's defiance as the problem.

The children felt put upon, pressured, rushed, and ignored. They didn't resist in order to *be* bad. They resisted because they *felt* bad. They resisted the demands of their parents' agendas which had no consideration for their own. But Ken and Melissa saw them as disobedient and unruly. So that is how they behaved. Their increasingly resistant behaviors signaled stress and tension.

Is Acceptance Unconditional?

Finn was a night owl, always had been. Mornings were like swimming through pudding for him. He wasn't pokey to make his mother mad; his body took longer to wake up. When Melissa thought about it, she realized the same was true of herself. Jake got locked in to television making it hard to get him to do what needed to be done. And time management did not come naturally. It wasn't that Jake was disobedient; it was that he wasn't a multitasker. It took learning about temperament to see that Natalie has always had a hard time with transitions. Her clinginess in the morning wasn't meant to drive her mother nuts; it was because she didn't want to feel the pain of saying goodbye.

Since being on time was their singular goal, Melissa and Ken were misinterpreting their children's behavior and sending messages that made things worse. In their frustration, they couldn't see that their three different children had three different coping strategies defending them against morning stress.

Are Expectations Set for Success or Failure?

Once they began working with the eight principles, Ken and Melissa realized they were setting their children up for failure because they were expecting the behavior that had been expected of them as children. But one parent was an only child, the other complied out of fear of an alcoholic father's unpredictability. Melissa recalled her father's label of "lazy" when she didn't follow his time clock. She realized she was labeling Finn with "pokey."

Tension was already in the air by the time they woke the children, each anticipating a morning battle. Their stern voices progressed to anger as soon as anyone didn't cooperate. They were always rushing. "Hurry up. How many times do I have to tell you to get dressed? Eat your breakfast, clean that up, turn the television off, brush your teeth, we're going to be late." Melissa expected that it was up to the children to make mornings easier. And Ken just wanted the children to obey. He felt tense whenever Melissa was angry, so he demanded that the children do as she say. He didn't realize he was asking them to take responsibility for her tension.

Is Connection Being Made?

For Ken and Melissa to connect, they had to be the first to change. First, to acknowledge that they were being disrespectful to the children with their criticisms. In order to do that, they needed to shift their perception to see that the children were *having* problems, not *being* problems. They had to give them a chance to be successful. They made a list of each of the hurdles they had to jump before getting out the door. They decided to start the day with smiles and hugs to see if that made a difference. They would need to get up fifteen minutes earlier to get themselves together before wake-ups.

Ken was gone by the time Natalie had to get up, so he woke the boys while Melissa finished her shower. They found it was better for one parent to handle wake-ups rather than both chiming from the doorway, "Come on, get up. It's late, gotta move!" Ken allowed ten minutes for wake-up time instead of calling from the door. Back rubs and soft voices got better responses. Finn was woken first so he had a chance to move slowly before Jake got up. Being on separate details reduced the stress and criticism between the parents. Melissa noticed that when she was in the kitchen with the kids, she became a time clock, stressing everyone starting with herself. So she focused on Natalie while the boys got their breakfast.

Once Melissa realized Natalie's problem, her frustration turned to compassion, and connection came easily. She shared with Natalie how much she hated to get out of bed and out the door in the mornings too. Natalie was amazed. "You do!" she said, feeling comforted to hear that she was not the only one to suffer this plague. "Yep, so I know just how you feel." Naming Natalie's transition difficulty from home to daycare helped Natalie feel normal, accepted, and understood. They talked about the good time she had once she got settled there and who she would see when she arrived. Together they worked out a game to play that motivated them both to get beyond their "morning problem," as they called it.

What Qualities Need Focus in Order to Grow?

Melissa looked for situations where she could point out to Natalie how easily she made changes—for instance, from the car into the building or from playing by herself to coming to dinner. And when dressing in the morning was particularly hard, Melissa paid extra attention helping her dress—no longer feeling manipulated.

Acknowledging that Finn was not a morning person and a slow mover meant anticipating his need for more time to do anything. Ken told him how lucky he was that he would never be a type A personality, frantically on the go, and how people would enjoy being around such a relaxed person. Feeling accepted meant that Finn no longer needed to resist. He actually started moving a bit faster.

Once Ken told Jake how much he admired his stick-to-itiveness, seeing something through to the finish, and his attention to details, he was in a better position to talk about the difficulty of getting out the door on time. They both agreed that he should have all his necessities done before he put his mind on what he wanted to do.

One evening at the end of dinner, Ken and Melissa decided together to tell them how proud they were of all their children for refusing to submit to the pressure and demands they had been faced with in the morning. All three stared as if their parents were aliens. Assuring them that they intended to change their tune, Melissa said, "We need to come up with a morning plan, and we need your help to do it." They were all ears. By owning their problem and no longer dumping it on the children, Ken and Melissa were able to connect. Cooperation was now possible.

How Can the Problem Be Solved Without Punishment?

Melissa and Ken made it clear that mornings needed to work for everyone. They first went over their prepared list of problems: Notices were left in the bottom of backpacks, lunch boxes were left with rotting food, library books were misplaced and late, homework was often forgotten, and breakfast in front of television led to battles. Melissa was late for work more often than not, and Ken left upset whenever there was yelling going on. Complaints from the children included feeling rushed, fighting over the bathroom, and yucky lunches. Over a few sessions after dinner, they worked out a contract they all agreed to, signed, and posted.

1. Basket in kitchen is for contents of backpacks that anyone else should see, homework that needs checking, papers to be signed, and library books.
2. Finn and Jake write a bathroom schedule for each weekday morning to be shown to parents and posted on bathroom door.
3. Lunch boxes are to be emptied into trash and sink after school or else the owner will clean out his own. If that doesn't happen, the owner receives no lunch.
4. Anyone unhappy with his lunch can place a request or make his own the night before. No changes made in the morning.
5. Clothes are picked out at night. Anyone is allowed to sleep in clothes for the following day as long as they are clean.
6. Melissa and Natalie get dressed together while boys get their breakfast.
7. Anyone missing the bus will have to drive by way of daycare first.
8. Natalie will go to daycare in pajamas with clothes in the car if she isn't dressed on time.
9. No TV in the morning.

Number nine was the only one the children hadn't co-authored and was the hardest for the children to accept. It caused a good deal of balking in the morning for about a week before they realized their complaints weren't going to change anything. Ken and Melissa stood firm but still connected. "Yeah, of course you're mad. You were used to TV for a long time and now we've stopped it. I'd be mad too if I were you" usually took the wind out of their angry sails.

Are Strong Boundaries Keeping Good Balance?

Melissa had blamed the kids for making her late, tense, and angry each morning. Ken blamed them whenever Melissa got upset. Peace had been left entirely up to the children—handed off as their problem to fix. But, it was not their responsibility. Getting up earlier helped Ken and Melissa to start the day in better balance. Nothing went as neatly as planned, but the difference was noticeable. The key was sticking to a routine and no one being asked to take responsibility for a problem that was not his. Given these boundaries, the children were more willing to help out when unforeseen problems inevitably arose. Mornings were generally calmer and much less frantic. Getting five people out of the house on time every morning was never easy, but it became a skirmish not a battle.

CHAPTER 10

Chores

My two children responded to chores as differently as day and night. My son has an easygoing temperament and rarely resisted what he was asked to do. He often procrastinated, but reminders would soon do the trick. But it was like pulling stale taffy to get my daughter on board. Maintaining my principles, I needed to take each of their styles into consideration and realize that just because they approached chores differently didn't mean they weren't both helping.

How Is the Behavior Intended for Success?

Being successful incorporates cooperation, the desire to help, and feeling confident and valued. Remember when your toddler wanted to do the dishes, cook, mow the lawn, use the tools, vacuum, load the dishwasher, and feed the animals? The desire to help, to chip in and be included, is innate—when it's fun and feels good. Young children are developmentally self-centered, but when their needs are fulfilled, they are also helpful and empathic. As this initial desire to help transforms into regular expected assistance, children gain self-discipline and responsibility. When they know they are counted on, they feel valued and important. Children who are not required to help feel less successful and have lower self-esteem. It is the transformation from fun to expected assistance that we can make or break.

Casey's pride in himself was evident when I overheard him and his friend bragging about who had the most chores. It was easy for him. Molly's resistance told me that it wasn't easy for her.

She had something going on that made it hard. I had to find out what that was. It wasn't that she didn't want to help.

What Is the Behavior Signaling?

Casey's accepting behavior was my green light to expect a lot. When he was in middle school, every morning he lit the wood-stove, took the dog for a walk and fed her, made his lunch, fixed his breakfast, and gave fresh water to the rabbit on his way to school. I had to be mindful that I was not expecting too much. My job with Molly was to find ways she could feel helpful without provoking further resistance. Her behavior was my yellow light to slow down and evaluate what I was asking of her.

Once chores feel like hard labor that come with punitive consequences of withholding allowance or privileges for not doing them, the innate desire to help is undermined. Molly's resistance told me she didn't like to work. But she did like feeling helpful. I had to find jobs that worked for her so she could feel helpful but not overwhelmed.

Is Acceptance Unconditional?

Casey was easygoing and cooperative; Molly was strong-willed, slow to transition, and never liked being told what to do. I had more success when I gave her time and didn't expect action right away. She showed less resistance to jobs that appealed to her creativity. She never minded setting and clearing the table. She took pride in arranging the colors of the plates and napkins and did it with her brother while we were all in the kitchen. She remembers fondly an extra job of stacking bricks for which she was paid a penny a brick. She liked feeling responsible for how the stack looked when the bricks were piled.

Appealing to what is natural in your child will help with unconditional acceptance. If your child is highly active, ask him to do something for you that requires speed. If he is artistic, he could pick out the bowls for food or make place mats or center-pieces. If he likes to read, ask him to read labels and prices at the grocery store.

Are Expectations Set for Success or Failure?

Just because Casey was more willing did not mean Molly should be too, or that there was something wrong with her. To set my children up for success meant that I had to keep my eye on the goal—for them both to feel important, cooperative, and valued. That did not mean they had to do the same things. For each of them to feel successful meant holding different expectations. It would have been easier to stop expecting anything from Molly and let her off the hook. But that expectation would have set her up for failure. I had to accept her complaints but still expect her help. When I expected her to groan and resist, it was easier to stop myself from reacting whenever she did.

Is Connection Being Made?

Allowing Molly to complain helped me connect with her. Once I acknowledged how much she didn't want to do something, her resistance dropped. Instead of many regular jobs, I often asked Molly in the moment to help me with something. That gave me the opportunity to show my appreciation. My language and tone of voice affected the amount of resistance I would get. I always asked myself, "If I were her, how would I like hearing what I'm saying?"

Listen to yourself:

- "No computer time until chores are finished."
  - Better: "I'd like you to clear the table and take out the trash before computer time."

- "Why can't you ever do what I ask?"
  - Better: "You really hate taking the trash out. It's a yucky job, and I so appreciate it when you help out with it."
- "No allowance for you this week."
  - Better: "I'll take you to your friends after you give me a hand with the dishes."
- "After all I've done for you, and you won't do this one thing for me."
  - Better: "I have a lot to do before we can leave. Would you rather bring the laundry down from upstairs or put the breakfast dishes in the sink while I write the grocery list?"

Molly always dug in her heels in reaction to a demand. Choices gave her power. "I need the dishes put in the dishwasher and the coats hung up, which would you rather do to help me out?" would usually get a positive response.

What Qualities Need Focus in Order to Grow?

Water your child's helpfulness like seeds. Build slowly and gently on your toddler's desire to help. Begin with things that you have noticed he enjoys. When you are vacuuming, let him push even if it takes more time for you to help him. Molly "helped" me fold laundry when she wanted to be with me. So doing her own laundry came easily for her.

Pay attention to whatever your child does on his own that is helpful. If he hands his sister something she asks for, note it, if only to yourself. Find those "islands of competency." Don't praise for carrying a grocery bag with, "Good for you. You're such a good helper," but do say, "Thanks, I appreciate your help. These bags are heavy."

How Can the Problem Be Solved Without Punishment?

If I had used coercion, everything I asked would have felt like a punishment. I looked for helping opportunities that were logical. A consequence led to a routine job for Casey. He rarely put his dirty clothes in the hamper or his clean clothes in his drawers regardless of how many times I reminded him. I told him that he would have to do his own laundry if his dirty clothes were not in the hamper the next laundry day. The day came and guess what? I took him and his clothes to the washing machine, gave him clear instructions, and set him to it. What I didn't expect was that he liked it and continued doing his own laundry from then on. Molly followed his lead and started doing hers soon after.

When resistance is too high, tell your child that you don't feel like taking him where he wants to go, since he didn't feel like helping you when you asked. Ask how you both can change that. Consequences work far better when they are logical and don't feel punitive or blaming.

Take the word "chore" out of your vocabulary. Talk to your children about helping out, lending a hand, chipping in, or doing a job. Don't read or watch television while your children are expected to work. If you work as a family, chores are easier to swallow. Plan something fun like getting ice cream or going for a bike ride as motivation for getting the family jobs done. But stay away from rewards or allowance conditional on a job done. Allowance is essential for teaching the value of money. It should not be used as a punishment or reward, both of which undermine that inherent desire to help.

Reevaluate jobs after a period of time and switch them so they don't get boring. Try picking up toys to clean-up music. Challenge them to basket tosses into a toy box. Ask your child to pick up the red toys while you pick up the green ones. Set up a job like room cleaning well ahead of time. Ask your child when would be the best time for him. Write it on the calendar. You will get less resistance than springing, "You've got to clean your room now. No playdates until it's done."

When resistance is high, problem-solve. "I'm having a problem because I'm not getting any help around the house. I cannot do everything. I want you to tell me what it is about helping you don't like." You will get more cooperation when there is no blame. Remember your goal is to grow helpfulness, not just get a job done.

Are Strong Boundaries Keeping Good Balance?

I had to be very careful never to ask Casey to compensate for his sister. Or compare them. If I had said to Molly, "Why can't you help like Casey does?" her resistance would have quickly turned to defiance and refusal. Household jobs are basically the parent's problem. Children need motivation and appreciation, not criticism, to help us with our problems. "It's your job to take the trash out. Now do it," lays your problem on your child, and it will not feel fair. Keeping that boundary clear and strong will help the resistant child meet you halfway. "The trash needs emptying. Do you want to do it now or after dinner?" keeps you out of the dictator role.

Don't do it all, and don't do your children's jobs when they resist unless a pet needs feeding. When you do, the message is loud and clear that you will do everything. So why should anyone else? Your resentment builds when no one helps. You create a dependency in your child when he knows you will end up doing it. And do not do it over. It's demeaning for a child who has put in time doing the dishes to get a roll of your eyes, a lecture on how to clean dishes, and then to watch you do them over.

Consider whether room cleaning is a battle worth fighting. Your child's room is his territory in what otherwise belongs entirely to adults. He is making his mark on that world by keeping his room different. One Saturday after Casey had cleaned his room, I went in to speak to him. All over the floor were tiny bits of paper, a toothpick, a paperclip. I began picking up the bits. He said, "Mom, what are you doing?" I said, "I'm just picking up all these little bits." He said, "But they're my little bits. I like them." Making children clean their rooms because you want them clean does not make logical sense to them. Appeal to their desire to cooperate as you state your problem—you don't want mice and insects coming for crumbs, you don't want to trip over on the way to kissing them goodnight, you want their help in keeping the house clean.

CHAPTER 11

Sibling Rivalry

Rebecca realized that she was on constant alert for fighting to break out between Jackson and Isabelle. It seemed that for the past four years since Isabelle's birth, Jackson, seven, has punched, shoved, or poked his sister every chance he got—often accompanied by a smirk or laughter. Isabelle would scream, Jackson would get yelled at for "knowing better," made to apologize, put in time-out, and Rebecca was left fearing she was raising a sociopath. The next day it would start again. But after hearing Jackson cry one night that nobody loved him, Rebecca knew something had to change.

How Is the Behavior Intended for Success?

Children do not want to hate each other or fight constantly. It's stressful. It may look as if Jackson enjoys plaguing his sister—his laughter makes Rebecca think so—but he is fighting for his life. Isabelle is a threat to him. His physical and verbal attacks—his attempts to gain power—signal powerlessness at its root. He is attempting to even the score to feel in balance with his sister.

Let's face it; siblings fight. They learn a lot about relationships through fighting. In a successful relationship, friendship and loyalty accompany sporadic fights. But when occasional punches turn to angry battles with hard slugs and abusive putdowns, an obstacle—in Jackson's case a belief that he is bad and his sister is good—displaces success. His mother's constant vigilance, punishments, and reprimands tell Jackson that he is not to be trusted, increasing his obstacle. His cry for help—claiming that no one loves him—indicates his need for acceptance. He is trying to tell his mother that he is not cruel and remorseless, rather than hurt and jealous.

What Is the Behavior Signaling?

Rebecca has taken Jackson's attacks at face value, missing the clues that jealousy and resentment are consuming him. "Nobody loves me" and "How come you never get mad at her?" are his fervent attempts to be heard. Jackson's problem has grown over four years from jealousy over a new baby to resentment of what he perceives to be preferential treatment. It is his perception that is the root that needs attending. His perception drives his behavior, not reality. Isabelle reminds him that she is the favorite every time he sees her. He has no choice but to defend himself. Laughter is one way. Seeing how mad it makes his mother, he clings to this weapon of power.

Is Acceptance Unconditional?

Rebecca often doesn't like Jackson. His behavior is unacceptable, but Rebecca equates his behavior with him. She believed her punishments would change his behavior, but all they did was make him feel unloved and no good.

Jackson had always been a physical child. As a toddler, he would tackle his mother at the back of her legs making her knees buckle. He went through a year of biting, causing Rebecca much anxiety. She didn't know that physical aggression can be inborn and doesn't turn violent unless it is mismanaged.

Isabelle was the adorable, blond, blue-eyed girl Rebecca always hoped for. From birth, she was the focus of attention. Every time Jackson was rough with her, he was scolded. "You're the big brother. You should know better than to hurt her"—even though big brother was only four, developmentally impulsive, and temperamentally physical. He never knew who his mother wanted him to be. All he knew was the threat he felt from his sister, who he was supposed to love.

Are Expectations Set for Success or Failure?

Rebecca was the youngest. She had two older brothers who taunted her constantly. She felt unprotected by an uninvolved, depressed mother. Rebecca identified with Isabelle from the beginning and was determined to give her the protection she never had. But her determination blinded her to Jackson's needs.

"Troublemaker" is what Jackson sees reflected in his mother's eyes, so he has come to expect it of himself. Feeling protected, Isabelle is free to provoke her brother all she wants. Her power is in getting Jackson in trouble by crying. Rebecca assumed that punishing Jackson and protecting Isabelle was her job. But she has set Isabelle up as the innocent victim to her brother, the bully.

Is Connection Being Made?

Rebecca hated the dislike she felt toward Jackson and sought counseling. She learned that behind his wall of defense, Jackson had no opportunity to experience remorse and no motivation to change his behavior. She needed to understand Jackson.

Being aggressive by nature, Jackson's impulses needed physical release—just not on Isabelle. Rebecca got him a punching bag for the playroom. Each time he reacted physically toward Isabelle, instead of yelling at him, she put the gloves on his hands and said, "Go hit the punching bag." She had to trust that giving him permission to hit was okay—just not a person. Sometimes she asked Jackson to draw how he felt about Isabelle. Hard scribbles of black and red told the story, and ripping up the paper helped with release. Afterwards Jackson seemed calmer. But sometimes the punching bag just didn't do it, and Rebecca wasn't always able to rechannel his energy. Sometimes she just blew up.

In order to connect, Rebecca had to break the bully/victim spell she had cast on them and address the roots, not just the behavior. She needed to find confidence in her children's ability to negotiate, compromise, and be kind. She needed to see them as she wanted them to see themselves.

What Qualities Need Focus in Order to Grow?

Since she got too mad at Jackson, it was easier to start by empowering Isabelle out of her victim role. She focused on Isabelle's capability.

The next time Isabelle complained that Jackson was mean to her, Rebecca tried her new skills. "You don't like it when Jackson hurts you. I don't blame you. Can you think of how to tell him?" When Isabelle insisted she couldn't, Rebecca added, "You are good at knowing what you want, Isabelle. I bet you'll be really good at telling Jackson to stop. What can you do if he doesn't listen?" Isabelle flopped to the floor and whined, "I can't. You have to." But Rebecca stuck with it, and after many ups and downs Isabelle slowly took up her arguments with Jackson. Rebecca helped but stopped doing it for her.

Kindness was what she wanted to grow in Jackson, so Rebecca put attention on how he dealt with their dog. "See how Finley seems to smile when you rub his belly so softly. Dogs love kindness, don't they?" And whenever he did something she asked, she thanked him for being kind. One day, she overheard Jackson saying "thanks" to Isabelle when he asked her to hand him the purple crayon. Rebecca knew it would take time for Jackson to see himself as kind, but he did seem more relaxed.

How Can the Problem Be Solved Without Punishment?

Rebecca worked hard at learning connective communication (detailed in Chapter 5) so she could support each of their strengths and stop playing favorites. But all they wanted to do was tell her why the other one should get in trouble. She first had to learn their game before she could step out of it.

The Triangle Game

Whenever parents accept the job of fixing sibling problems, they get sucked into the Triangle Game.

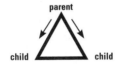

A. Children direct complaints to parent

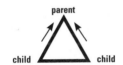

B. Parent deflects complaints back to children

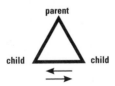

C. Children communicate complaints to each other

When the children's accusations were directed to her (A), Rebecca thought she had to solve the problem. They each wanted her to rule in their favor and fought hard to make that happen. "Jackson hit me." "She started it." All of it went to Rebecca. Like a coach who tosses the ball back into the game, Rebecca had to break the triangle by tossing the ball back to them (B), encouraging them to tell each other what their problem was (C). Tossing the ball back meant that Rebecca would no longer play judge and jury but merely sounding board. So to "Jackson pushed me," Rebecca would respond empathically, "I bet you didn't like that. You need to tell him, not me." And to, "She asked for it. She is such a jerk," Rebecca would reply, "Tell Isabelle why you think she asked for it. She needs to hear that." Eventually they learned that their mother listened but wasn't going to help.

Conflict Resolution

Breaking free of the Triangle Game set Rebecca up for resolving the conflict. Assuring them that no one was going to get in trouble or lose, she brought them together so they could tell each other their gripes. She stopped any interrupting, reminding them they would each get their turn to tell their side. After they had gotten everything out, she asked what they wanted to do about it. Rebecca empathized with or validated each and then encouraged and facilitated their communication.

"You sound really angry about Isabelle going in your room. What do you want to say to her?"

And then, "Isabelle, can you agree to what Jackson has asked for?"

"So Isabelle agrees to stay out of your room but still wants to play with your things. What do you think about that?"

"Jackson sounds pretty mad about you messing up his game, Isabelle. What do you think he needs to hear from you?"

"So how do you both want to handle this problem so it won't happen again?"

Rebecca became a neutral guide gently leading them to find their own solutions. If they weren't cooperative or couldn't agree, Rebecca would table it and come back to it later until they all agreed on how the problem would get resolved. After a particularly difficult problem, they wrote a contract similar to the examples you saw in Chapter 7 about what was acceptable between them and what was not. One day, Rebecca reached her goal. She overheard Jackson say, "Be quiet, Isabelle, so Mommy doesn't come in and make us talk about it."

The Steps of Conflict Resolution

1. Parent is coach, not judge. Be objective, detached, and neutral. Do not direct, criticize, or blame. This is your children's problem, not yours.
2. Remind children that no one will get in trouble, no one will lose.
3. Tell them to tell each other their complaints, not you.
4. Give them each uninterrupted turns to tell their side of the story.
5. Facilitate the problem solving with questions or empathizing comments.
6. Offer suggestions but do not control the outcome.
7. Make lists of all suggestions, no matter how trite or unacceptable. Check off ones you cannot all agree on. You always have veto power.
8. All must agree on the final solution.
9. Write a contract if necessary.

The No-Blame Solution

After learning the No-Blame Solution, Rebecca understood that when blame is involved, something or someone else is always responsible. Defense is the only option when anyone feels accused. It took a huge leap of faith, but Rebecca had nothing to lose.

After Jackson returned from school one day, Isabelle wanted him to play penguins. He was telling her what a "jerky" game that was when Rebecca called for someone to let the dog out. Isabelle shrieked, "I will!" and Jackson yelled, "You always do it." Isabelle ran to open the door, but Jackson blocked it, shoving her out of the way. Isabelle fell backward, hit her head on the floor, and screamed. Rebecca came running. She stopped herself from yelling at Jackson while comforting Isabelle. Jackson ran out the door with the dog, anticipating his mother's blame.

Rebecca noticed how much Isabelle wanted Jackson to get in trouble. "Jackson knocked me down when I tried to open the door for Finley. He's so mean." She continued to comfort Isabelle until the crying subsided, not mentioning Jackson's name. It was hard but the lesson was fresh in her mind. She was aware that Jackson was lurking around the porch. "Jackson," she called, "would you like to get the ice pack from the freezer to hold on Isabelle's head?" He didn't answer but hung around while Rebecca got it. She wanted to scream at him, but she had learned that he would eventually want to make amends when he trusted he wouldn't be blamed or punished. She had her doubts.

After dinner while Isabelle was in the tub, Rebecca tried the next step. She connected with Jackson. "You must have felt pretty angry at Isabelle this afternoon. It's gotta be hard when she wants her way." He replied, "She always gets what she wants." Instead of saying, "No, she doesn't" and trying to teach him a lesson, she acknowledged how unfair that must feel. (Note: empathizing does not say that Isabelle does get what she wants.) Jackson was quiet. "I wonder if there was another way you could have let Finley out," she offered without a question. "She wouldn't let me." Bravely, Rebecca asked, "Do you think you're always going to let her get her way?" Surprised by his mother's question, Jackson said, "I could put my foot down, block the door, and tell her I'm doing it this time."

Rebecca was astonished. Jackson felt heard. The next time Rebecca suggested the ice pack, Jackson got it. No blame had been issued. He could experience remorse without shame. The fighting by no means stopped, but they were on their way.

Are Strong Boundaries Keeping Good Balance?

Sibling fights are the siblings' problem. In order to help her children, Rebecca had to let go of trying to fix their problems and taking responsibility for what was theirs. She recognized that the more she tried to solve their fights, the more critical and controlling she became, then the more punitive she had to be, and the more the children became dependent on her to end their battles. The hardest part was letting go of how things would turn out. She had to trust. Once she began to let go of controlling their problems, she could help each one be the person they needed to be—strong and confident. No blame, no defenses, no retaliation was the end result.

CHAPTER 12

Peer Pressure

Eleven-year-old Connor seemed different this year. His usual enthusiasm about school had always occupied dinner conversation. But fifth grade in the middle school, although new and exciting in September, even into October, had seemed to intimidate him into quietness of late. Connor's teasing and put-downs of his six-year-old sister, Chloe, had intensified beyond their normal love/hate relationship. School mornings were iffy as to whether or not Connor would be complaining of a stomachache. For the first time, Nancy didn't know how to manage her normally pleasant son.

How Is the Behavior Intended for Success?

Connor had always been cheerful, fun loving, and enthusiastic. Now he moped and spent more time in his room. He rarely shared his feelings openly so questions about what was going on got "Nothing" in reply. He did well in school and in sports. He had several good friends, some of whom he had known all through school. Wilson was his best friend. But Nancy hadn't seen him around lately—none of his friends, actually. She hadn't thought anything of it until Connor's behavior changed.

Connor had always been sensitive to disappointing his parents or doing anything to cause them more worry. His father, Paul, had been sick throughout Connor's early childhood, and then his parents divorced when he was seven. Connor never wanted to make further waves. He did his best to be a "good" boy and keep out of trouble. His silence was intended to keep his problems to himself and his parents free of worry. But his treatment of Chloe and isolating himself were his giveaways.

What Is the Behavior Signaling?

Nancy learned from Connor's doctor that stomachaches often signaled stress but that there was nothing physically wrong. A few more notes than usual were coming home from Mrs. Tilton. His work was showing minor decline and some homework assignments were missing but nothing serious. Paul hadn't noticed anything different and thought Nancy was overreacting.

The more Nancy nagged her son and asked what was wrong, the quieter he became. Her worry made any reassurances sound phony, and she sermonized about spending more time on homework and getting more organized. Mostly he didn't respond but once exploded with, "Stop talking about it. Leave me alone, I'm fine, okay?" He didn't know how to ask for what he didn't know he needed. He just felt mad and his behavior was disturbing. Nancy had to find out why.

Is Acceptance Unconditional?

Connor had always been sensitive. Firm words felt like rough sandpaper, as did seams in socks and new clothes. Too much stimulation easily overwhelmed him. Trips to the supermarket often provoked tantrums and leaving without groceries. As he got older, his sensitivity mellowed, but now he seemed more sensitive than ever, and Nancy quickly fell back into old patterns. She had always walked on eggshells around his sensitive nature with apologies and reassurances whenever he seemed offended, but now she wondered if she hadn't hardened him up enough. Had her carefulness given him permission to climb into a shell when things weren't going right? He seemed too young to be hitting adolescent withdrawal. She didn't know where to let go and where to intervene. Paul was no help. He always thought she overreacted.

Are Expectations Set for Success or Failure?

Because Connor had always been an adaptable, cooperative child, Nancy and Paul held high expectations of him. Connor rarely argued about what he was asked to do. He did chores like a trooper and included Chloe in his play whenever his mother insisted. He usually rose to any occasion as long as he didn't feel yelled at. Paul and Nancy had no idea that he was so sensitive to their problems, which they tried to keep from their children. It was clear to them that Connor was amenable and capable.

So when Paul decided to give Connor a computer for his eleventh birthday, he knew he could set some parameters around it by letting his son know that with the computer privilege came monitoring of his emails. Connor agreed. But when problems first arose for him, he felt alone. He feared his mother would freak out if he told her what was happening. It seemed far safer to keep things to himself. After all, he knew how capable he was at helping others, so why wouldn't he be able to help himself? He didn't realize that his problems were leaking into his behavior.

Is Connection Being Made?

Nancy learned in her parenting class how much a boy like Connor needed a neutral sounding board in order to open up. Questions, especially lately, made him clam up. She had to put her worry aside and respond neutrally, so Connor would trust her enough to open up. With encouragement and support from her class, she stopped asking him questions about what was wrong and structured homework time and studying as if nothing had changed. She tried the No-Blame Solution (see Chapter 11) for sibling fights, but Nancy could tell the root was still there.

Sometimes when stomachaches were bad he stayed home, and sometimes she insisted he go.

Finally, it seemed time to try her new connective communication skills. The next time she was driving him to an away basketball game she gave it a go.

"You know, Connor, I've noticed that you've been spending a lot of time alone in your room. I'm just a bit confused by that since I don't know whether that means you just want more privacy or you're angry with me or Chloe."

"Privacy."

Nancy didn't know where to go now and was sorry she'd given him the privacy out. She tried again in a few minutes, "You also seem sadder to me than you used to."

Connor looked out the window. Nancy waited a few minutes and then changed the subject.

"What's Wilson been up to these days?"

"How should I know?" Connor's angry tone of dismissal was the clue Nancy needed. She chose her words and her tone carefully so as not to react with her usual worry.

"Oh. Sounds like you had a falling out."

"He's a jerk."

Nancy bit her tongue to keep from saying, "You shouldn't call your friends a jerk."

"So I guess he's not your best friend anymore."

"I don't know. I don't want to talk about it."

Nancy dropped it, but she had learned a major clue. She called Paul that night after Connor was in bed. Paul said he hadn't monitored Connor's incoming emails for a couple of months and would do so. The next night he told Nancy what he had learned. A boy named Arty had been emailing Connor hate notes. Paul read some to Nancy: "You know everyone at school says you're a faggot." "Your mother is screwing the gym teacher." "You're a f...ing loser." "Nobody likes you. You're going down."

What now? Horrified, they decided that Paul would confront Connor that weekend when he had the kids. Nancy would take Chloe Saturday afternoon. She desperately wanted to call the school, but Paul convinced her that could make things worse for Connor. She had to be patient.

What Qualities Need Focus in Order to Grow?

Connor needed to know that letting his parents in was more important than worrying them. Paul knew that Connor's silence about the emails meant that he didn't know how to tell them, not that he was being sneaky and deceitful. He would need to focus on his son's consideration of them rather than his anger at not being told.

Before he launched into the emails, he decided to share a story with Connor of a time he had been bullied in fourth grade by a new kid in school. Connor seemed very interested but offered nothing.

Then Paul said, "Connor, I checked your emails a couple of nights ago." Connor's face froze. "Do you remember we had a deal about that when I gave you the computer?" Connor nodded his head then dropped it to his chest.

"I think I know how hard it must be for you to talk to us because you don't want us to worry. And you probably figure that you can handle this yourself. You're a very capable, strong kid." Connor raised his head. "Who is this Arty?" his father continued.

The story came out. Arty, a new boy at school, was trying to gather friends wherever he could and had targeted the very popular Wilson as one of them. Arty knew that Wilson and Connor were best friends and had begun his campaign to turn Wilson against Connor. He had "bought" Wilson with some prize baseball cards and an invitation to a ballgame with him and his dad and two other friends of Connor's. Since then, Wilson had seemed friendly enough but never suggested getting together after school. Connor noticed him hanging out with Arty during recess. Paul conjectured that part of Arty's efforts was to silence Connor by humiliating him. Connor began to cry.

How Can the Problem Be Solved Without Punishment?

In discussing how to handle the situation, Paul and Nancy knew that if they had reprimanded Connor for not telling them about the emails, they could have pushed him further into isolation. He would have felt accused and misunderstood. They would have to be careful not to react and tell him what to do, but to support him in doing what he thought best. Supporting him was their job, carrying it out was his.

Once everything was out in the open, Nancy continued her connective communication with Connor by acknowledging the pain he must be in and the tension he must feel from having kept it in so long. The more upset her tone, the less he connected. She needed to be a sounding board and a good listener once she empathized and validated Connor's feelings. As much as she was tempted to tell him what to do and say to this Arty, who brought out her killer instinct, and as much as she wanted to call this boy and run the riot act to his mother, Nancy knew that she would only infuriate her son. He had gone this long in silence, which told her he wasn't asking for help. Even though she knew he needed it, she wanted him to do the problem solving.

"So Connor, if you could say anything you wanted to Arty, what might it be?" she ventured.

"Lay off and find your own friends." It seemed that Connor cared more about losing Wilson than Arty's harassment.

"And what do you wish you could say to Wilson?"

"I don't know. If he doesn't want to be friends, I guess that's his decision."

"Oh, so you're willing to let him go that easily?" Nancy challenged. "I would have thought he meant more to you."

Connor let down. "He does, but I don't know what to do about it." He started to tear up.

Nancy asked if she could make a suggestion, as he seemed truly stuck. He said yes.

"What if you told him about the emails you had been getting? What do you think he would say?"

"He probably wouldn't believe me."

"But what if he did? How will you know, if you don't try?"

Connor said he would think about it. Nancy said that she would help in any way. Later that day, Nancy suggested, "What if you made copies of them and put them in an envelope with a letter to Wilson? He'd have to believe you then."

Connor did make copies but found his own way to present them to Wilson. Once he had his parents' support but not their worry that he was some kind of victim, he found the courage. Wilson was soon hanging around the kitchen.

Are Strong Boundaries Keeping Good Balance?

Nancy had to let go of her own agenda, her conviction that she had to handle it. She had to be willing to let him find his own way. When she asked about talking to his teacher, he said an emphatic no. Nancy had learned about the difference between her problem and her child's. As distraught as she was, she knew that this was Connor's problem. It didn't mean that she had to leave him to fend for himself. It meant that she had to help him find his way through it without imposing her way to try to fix it.

Once his mother and father's support enabled him to act, they could highlight his courage and resilience. Connor emerged stronger than before.

CHAPTER 13

Homework

Fourth-grader Jocelyn had always been developmentally behind her peers in most areas, but with her mother's diligent effort to get effective services, she had caught up about a year ago. Although a competent reader and speller, conceptualizing and comprehending does not come easily. Getting it done, not getting it right, is Jocelyn's motto. She is usually a B-/C student but gets her share of Ds. She claims she will do better next time, but when next time comes, she insists she doesn't care about grades. Homework time is a nightmare for Harriet, her single mother. "I'm not a slave driver," she said, "but I go ballistic when I hear her say, 'I don't care!'"

How Is the Behavior Intended for Success?

Anyone would think that Jocelyn doesn't care about being successful. She makes up answers just to get homework done and shows no concern if it's not finished. But Jocelyn's attitude is a cover-up for insecurity—her obstacle—that she expresses as indifference. Inferiority equals failure to Jocelyn. Her "I don't care" approach may be her best effort toward success in a realm where she can barely keep her head above water.

Little children are sponges for learning. "Wha's dat?" and "Why?" make up much of a toddler's vocabulary. Exhausted parents can't teach them enough. But when learning becomes mandatory and formatted, some children don't fit the format, and enthusiasm dries up. Jocelyn has lost almost all of hers. But

Harriet must keep her focus on Jocelyn's innate desire to learn and do well that lies beneath the obstacle in Jocelyn's way. That desire has been eroded and needs attention—and possibly a different format.

What Is the Behavior Signaling?

Apathy and anger, seen on the surface, are Jocelyn's defense strategies protecting deeper feelings of frustration and fear. She will refuse to do homework, scream names at her mother, have an all-out tantrum, or rip up assignment papers. "She won't take the time to think anything through," Harriet complained, "and when she hits that wall of intolerance, there is no way to get her back on track." Her behaviors are distressing but signal a deeper problem than anger and apathy. Jocelyn is not lazy or a failure. She is hurting inside. Threats of bad grades or missing recess mean nothing to her because in her mind she is already a failure. So she says she doesn't care. She feels more in control of that. Harriet takes her at her word.

Childology, outlined in Chapter 2, tells it differently. Knowing that words are not always meant but intended to get or deflect attention, Jocelyn's "I don't care" might be interpreted as "nobody cares about me because I'm stupid." She successfully deflects her shame over feelings of inadequacy and saves face with indifference and haughtiness.

Is Acceptance Unconditional?

Harriet couldn't get enough of academia. It's hard for her to understand another attitude. She thinks that if only Jocelyn worked harder she would learn to enjoy it too. But Jocelyn is a different kind of thinker. School is her nemesis. Getting homework over with as quickly as possible, wrong answers and all, is her agenda.

Successful students use grades as motivators, but unsuccessful students live in a mindset that Dr. Martin Seligman, professor of psychology at the University of Pennsylvania, calls "learned helplessness." No matter how much time and effort they spend, they know they can't succeed. Nagging, critical parents unintentionally feed into this mindset, sending messages that their children are lazy and don't measure up. Jocelyn fell into a state of learned helplessness when learning delays placed her behind her peers. Catching up did not erase that mindset.

Horses are Jocelyn's love and lifeline. Unfortunately, Harriet has used them to motivate, taking away riding privileges if homework is not finished. Withholding Jocelyn's main source of self-confidence and competence pulled the rug out from underneath her and increased her obstacle.

Are Expectations Set for Success or Failure?

Harriet assumed that her daughter would be the academic star that both she and her older sons had been. The only one in her family to attend college, let alone accomplish a master's degree, Harriet views education as the road to independence and set high academic standards on all her children. Being a single mother and a high achiever, Harriet is out to prove that it can be done.

Jocelyn's learning delays initially posed a threat to Harriet's goals. Harriet fought hard to get services in place, worked overtime with Jocelyn at home, and told her daughter daily that she could do it. Harriet's best intentions got Jocelyn caught up but prevented her from seeing her daughter's real needs. Her expectations were set appropriately for her sons but not for Jocelyn, who knew she could never be the student her mother wanted.

Is Connection Being Made?

Harriet assumed that spending time with her daughter and helping with homework was the connection she needed. But whenever she focused on what Jocelyn was doing wrong, the connection was broken. The more Harriet strived to help, the more Jocelyn felt nagged and inadequate. Once Harriet understood how her expectations were being received, she pulled back and began hunting for roots. Even though she no longer saw Jocelyn's early delay as a problem, she now appreciates that Jocelyn experienced feeling "dumb" for a long time—something she still calls herself. She also calls her mother "stupid," a projection of her own feelings, when Harriet tells her how to do her homework.

Using connective communication (see Chapter 5), Harriet can acknowledge how hard it must be living in the shadow of her academic brothers and mother. "I wonder if you feel that no one in this family gets you and what you want" is a good guess and would likely initiate the release of some anger and frustration. Once Harriet can stop feeling responsible for Jocelyn's homework, she will be able to genuinely empathize with her and talk about how she learns differently, not poorly. But Harriet must connect with the daughter she has, not the daughter she wishes for.

What Qualities Need Focus in Order to Grow?

If Harriet can focus on the islands of Jocelyn's competence and let up on homework—at least temporarily—the mirror Jocelyn looks into will change. Harriet began by reminding herself that Jocelyn's homework problems do not make her a less capable person. It simply means she hates homework. Since she is good at reading and spelling, Harriet can build on those strengths, thus building her confidence, by asking her to write grocery lists, read labels, compare prices, and advise her mother about best buys. She can put more attention on Jocelyn's riding skills, ask more about her riding practices, look to her as the horse "expert," choose books about horses and read them together. Comments like, "I really admire your love of animals. You seem to have a real connection with that horse" can go a long way in competence building.

How Can the Problem Be Solved Without Punishment?

But Jocelyn still needs to do homework. "What's left if I can't withhold something she cares about?" indicates that Harriet still sees Jocelyn's behavior as a problem to be punished. In his groundbreaking book, *The Homework Myth: How Our Children Are Getting Too Much of a Bad Thing*, Alfie Kohn argues that homework actually undermines and inhibits a child's innate desire to learn—certainly true of children like Jocelyn. Changes in schools' homework expectations will be a long time coming, but this understanding can help shift Harriet's thinking and perhaps reduce the anxiety that fuels the homework situation.

Jocelyn needs to feel more in control. Harriet found that by asking her to choose the best time for homework, together with words like, "What do you need in order to...?" worked well most of the time. Jocelyn decided to get homework over with right after school. Even though she was tired and didn't focus well, Harriet let go of Jocelyn doing her best in favor of at least doing it—for now. Taking breaks didn't work for Jocelyn, since she resisted stretching the time out any longer than she had to. Instead, Harriet imposed breaks by telling her to keep working while she fixed them each a cup of tea with biscuits.

There was less screaming and name-calling when Harriet stopped punishing, threatening, or taking away privileges. She also ignored complaints, grumblings, and pounding of fists, and responded only to name-calling. "Don't you dare talk to me like that" changed to, "I'm not stupid and neither are you. I won't let anyone call me that, and I hope you won't either. You just don't like homework. That's understandable." Period.

Harriet needed to trust that once Jocelyn's obstacle was attended to, natural consequences would help the process. When Jocelyn put off her hardest assignment to the last possible evening and then complained she wouldn't have time to do it all, Harriet said calmly while biting her tongue, "You can either do it now before bed, in the morning, or not at all, it's your choice." Jocelyn raised her eyebrows. "But if it's unfinished or not done, it still needs to be included in your folder." When bedtime came, Jocelyn decided she would do it in the morning. Morning came, and she haphazardly filled in a couple of the problems. She was angry about the whole thing but included the unfinished sheets. Harriet took Jocelyn's anger as a good sign—better than indifference. She had to let go and trust that when she handed over responsibility, the consequences would eventually have an effect. When Jocelyn got an incomplete, Harriet asked, "What's your plan now?" After more grumbling, Jocelyn said, "I'll do the hardest parts first."

The responsibility really shifted when Jocelyn and Harriet designed a self-evaluation to accompany each assignment. Her teacher had come up with the idea but suggested a check-plus or minus system for Harriet to score Jocelyn's work. It only fueled their battles. It kept Harriet in control, and whenever she awarded a check-minus, it felt like a punishment. By reworking the main idea, and handing the process over to Jocelyn, they got far better results.

Jocelyn's evaluation

Circle 1 for not at all, and 5 for very much:				
I learned from doing this assignment	1	2	3	4	5
This assignment was interesting to me	1	2	3	4	5
I gave this assignment my full attention	1	2	3	4	5
I did my best on this assignment	1	2	3	4	5

When children evaluate their own strengths and weaknesses, they become problem-solvers. But they must learn from their own mistakes in order to take responsibility for their work. So Harriet had to stay out of Jocelyn's evaluation. For the first week, Jocelyn circled only ones before putting real thought to it. Any shift to a two was encouraging, and after awhile a few threes got circled.

Ideas to Encourage Homework Initiative

- Allow your child to determine her regular homework time and place.
- Decide together on a reminder word you can use. Give it once.
- Be nearby and available for help during designated homework times.
- Offer tea or some other comfort during homework time.
- Require homework to be done during designated times. If it's not, it is handed in unfinished.
- Allow griping and anger without changing the rules.
- Allow the school to handle consequences.

- Never watch television or play games during homework time. Pay bills, do chores, etc.
- Talk about assignments, discuss subjects, and be involved but don't correct unless your child wants you to.
- Write up a homework contract if necessary.

Are Strong Boundaries Keeping Good Balance?

Harriet was beginning to experience the relief of letting go and turning over the homework responsibility to Jocelyn. The more she relaxed, the more Jocelyn relaxed. Letting go of possible school failure was a tough call, but it made it easier for Harriet to be a help, not a hindrance. The hard part was allowing and surviving the meltdowns and frustration without taking them personally.

Much as she hated it, Jocelyn had grown dependent on her mother for getting her work done. She knew her mother would make her do it. But when she couldn't make it all right, Jocelyn grew belligerent—learned helplessness. Finally she began to depend on herself.

CHAPTER 14

Mealtime

By the time Owen turned three, mealtimes were fraught with shrieking, name-calling, throwing food, refusing to eat, and running around. Banishment to a room occurred at least every other night. Spencer, seven, had always been a good eater, but Owen, now four, ate little, complaining that it made him "gag-choke." Their father, Nick, was a stickler for table manners, and Margaret was desperately worried about Owen's poor eating. Mealtime had become less consistent as Nick irregularly worked later hours and Margaret was overwhelmed with trying to maintain a schedule of any kind. Mealtime had become the most dreaded time of day for all of them.

How Is the Behavior Intended for Success?

Dinnertime is the hub of a family. Children love being with their parents. Success here can be easy—unless it's not. When Spencer was their only child, Nick worked nine to five, schedules were consistent, and dinnertime was smooth. Spencer craved the time with his dad and got wrapped up in telling the details of his day. Remaining at the table, being engaged, and eating were never issues for Spencer.

Owen was a fussy eater from the beginning, causing Margaret much anxiety, prompting her to bribes and following him around the house for "just one more bite." The more Margaret enforced eating, the more Owen ignored her or resisted. The messages he got about eating compounded his own "problem" or unique eating style. Sitting at the table is difficult for him. To feel better, he avoids it as much as possible.

What Is the Behavior Signaling?

"Stupid butt-face" was Owen's favorite expression whenever his brother looked at him sideways. Sitting together at the dinner table under his parent's scrutiny encouraged Owen's goading—anything to avoid the food issue. Sometimes Spencer would laugh, which got Owen giggling enough to fall off his chair. Sometimes Spencer would get angry and throw something at him. Nick and Margaret spent dinnertime yelling at them to stop and threatening no dessert or TV.

The cycle of misbehavior and angry reactions had created hard-to-break mealtime patterns. As Nick and Margaret began to understand in their parenting class that the boys were not a menace to society but were in fact signaling a problem that needed addressing, they started looking deeper. The boys' disruptions reflected their lack of engagement at mealtime, inconsistent scheduling, and the barrage of parental attacks. Their actions couldn't change until Margaret and Nick changed theirs.

Owen's refusal to eat and constant activity to and mostly from the table was due in part to his active temperament as well as the pressure on him to eat. The boys simply wanted to have fun. It often got out of hand. They weren't being bad; they were reacting to parents telling them they were bad.

Is Acceptance Unconditional?

From the beginning, Owen ran instead of walked. It seemed he could trip over the grain in the wood floor. By three, he had fifteen stitches in various places. His focus was distractible, making it hard for him to finish anything he started. Nick insisted on a calm, polite child at the dinner table. Owen couldn't be that child. Nick was sure that Spencer would return to normal if he could manage Owen. Owen saw that Spencer was his father's favorite, and that he was a problem. He reacted by showing off.

Even though Owen had always been a picky eater, disliking everything but white carbohydrates, he was often shamed for not eating. "You're going to shrivel up like a pea and then how will you like it?" "Look at your brother. He's not afraid to try things." He knew he wasn't okay unless he was more like his brother.

Are Expectations Set for Success or Failure?

Margaret was brought up in a home where expectations were set at an adult comfort level. Mealtimes required polite, quiet behavior, perfect table manners, clean plates, and asking to be excused. Nick used the term "tidy" to describe his dinnertimes. Utensils were used properly, fingers were never allowed, and no food particles touched the table or floor.

Even though Margaret and Nick were determined to make mealtimes more relaxing than theirs had been, the standards they had lived with creeped in. Margaret did not expect a clean plate, but she did insist on two bites of everything. The more she insisted, the less Owen complied, then the more frustrated she got. Nick expected sitting in chairs throughout the meal. Expectations were unrealistic for Owen to enjoy mealtime. His stress provoked mischievous behavior. To enforce their unrealistic standards, Nick and Margaret had no choice but to be mealtime police.

Is Connection Being Made?

As much as Margaret wanted Owen to eat, she wanted him to enjoy being at the table. But dinnertime was often prefaced by Margaret's abrupt demand to come to the table, angrily shutting off the television, and instigating a meltdown from Owen.

One night, Margaret heard herself at the table. "Stop messing around and sit. Take that napkin off your head. Stop making those noises. Don't put your fingers in your milk. Don't you dare throw that roll. Stop being silly and sit still. There will be no dessert until those vegetables are gone. Why can't we ever have a peaceful meal?" Everything was negative and demanding. She reacted to the boys' shouting by shouting at them. Connection was nonexistent. She got it that dinnertime was a chore to get through. She had to let go.

Margaret decided to focus on staying calm and trying a sense of humor. Something like "Mean ol' Mom requests your presence at the table. RSVPs kindly appreciated" got their attention enough to find out what or who had replaced their mother. She enlisted Nick in her experiment, and they decided their initial goal was to let the kids have fun, intervening only when necessary. Instead they watched and listened. Ironically, as Nick stopped harping on Owen to sit still, Spencer took on the job. Allowing Owen to stand or come and go, they saw that he lasted for longer stretches and come back more often.

What Qualities Need Focus in Order to Grow?

Once they recognized it was their expectations that needed changing, Margaret and Nick focused on what was already there. Spencer had always been a great conversationalist. They decided to watch for it's reemergence and encourage it. Although most of what he said was in reaction to Owen, they listened carefully for mention of a friend, school, or interest. Then one would jump in with, "So has Kirby called you about this weekend?" "What was your assembly about today?" "How's that video game working out?" If they tried to initiate conversation, they were ignored, but if they took their cues from what the boys said, conversation actually followed.

Nick convinced Margaret to stop fixing separate meals for Owen. She needed to see him as an able, albeit light, eater who would not starve.

It was clear that directions needed to be more positive. This took skill and practice for them both to be consistent. Eventually, "Stop hitting" changed to "Owen, what is your fist trying to say to Spence? It looks pretty mad. Give it words, not slugs." "Get to your room right now" became "You can either stop doing that or go in the other room. Your choice." "Get that napkin off your head" was reframed to "Napkins belong in laps." One night feeling relaxed, Nick mimicked Owen and put his own napkin on his head without a word. The boys stopped, looked at him, and burst into laughter. It led to all napkins on heads, more laughter, and some real fun.

How Can the Problem Be Solved Without Punishment?

Margaret and Nick actually made an appointment with each other to discuss strategies. The first thing they decided was to move dinner to the table instead of the kitchen counter where eye contact was difficult. They agreed on a consistent dinnertime as often as possible, whether or not Nick was home. They committed to positive directions, and when they slipped, they would later discuss with each other what could have been said differently. It was agreed there would be no adult conversation that did not include the boys. No punishments were used, but consequences gave a choice about stopping a behavior or leaving the table. As dinnertime became more enjoyable, the choice was easy. Dessert was not to be used as a punishment or reward.

Just talking about a plan helped them both shift out of bad habits. Then the plan went to the boys. They agreed to set the table after Margaret agreed to wait until their 5:30 program was over. They put candles on the table, one for each family member.

Each of them lit a candle for another, and someone always lit a candle for Nick if he wasn't there.

Bickering and silliness continued, but as expectations changed and consistency took over, behavior became more tolerable. When attention was taken off food and what or how much was eaten and put onto conversation and games like I Spy, the enjoyment factor rose. The more the boys were allowed to have fun, inappropriate play—fingers in the milk, spitting out food, toilet jokes—gradually ceased.

Margaret stopped being Owen's short-order cook. She always included something he would eat, often only bread. She tried to get a good snack into him in the afternoon and supplemented with vitamins. Margaret felt worn down by Owen's complaint that she was now "starving him," but Nick helped her stay the course.

Margaret prepared food in bowls so the boys could help themselves rather than handing them a full plate—loaded with expectations. Getting to scoop out his own food motivated Owen to put it on his plate. It rarely reached his mouth, but it was a step in the right direction. Margaret's rule for herself was never to mention food at the table.

Spencer actually became an eating role model for Owen. He would dare Owen to try something. Owen often rose to the challenge. Utensils of toothpicks and chopsticks brought more challenge, and once a month, on a night when Nick worked late, they had "no hands at the table" night. Margaret prepared chunky food, and everyone had to keep their hands behind their backs.

Are Strong Boundaries Keeping Good Balance?

Margaret and Nick's responsibility was buying food and preparing it. It ended there. The boy's responsibility was eating what and how much they wanted. Keeping those responsibilities separate was difficult for Margaret. Battles over begging for junk food ended when junk food was no longer purchased. When desserts became healthy food, it no longer mattered what had been eaten prior.

Having only healthy food in the house was a difficult change for the boys. Their demands and complaints were hard for Margaret. She took them as a personal attack. Sometimes she gave in and bought what they wanted to stop the arguing, but she knew if she wanted to make the plan work, she had to expect arguments, respect their right to complain, be a sounding board, yet stick to the plan. She needed regular reassurance from Nick. The hard part for Nick was allowing Owen to come and go at the table and to loosen his table manner standards. But as Owen hung around more, Nick felt encouraged.

As for Owen, it would likely be years before his eating habits would tolerate many foods, but seeing him relax and enjoy being together at the table was the reward they were after. Owen had learned that his mother was in charge of his food intake, so he had relinquished all responsibility for eating. Now he was given that responsibility.

With hard work and consistency, several months later Nick and Margaret realized they had reached their goal. They all looked forward to sitting around the table together.

CHAPTER 15

Bedtime

The Goreski family was exhausted. Nate, six, was still having daily temper tantrums, while Shawna, three, still had not slept through the night. Everything started falling apart in the late afternoon. Nate's soccer practice and music lessons threw off mealtimes and bedtimes three nights a week, and Shawna had to go along. Nate often got so wound up by five o'clock that his parents, Steven and Marcia, nicknamed him the "Energizer bunny." Shawna caught Nate's frenzy and the two of them seemed to bounce off each other. By the time bedtime rolled around, threats were flying, tears were spilled, and no one was happy. Disrupted sleep kept emotions on edge all day. Marcia was worn to a frazzle.

How Is the Behavior Intended for Success?

Neither Shawna nor Nate chose to wind up and provoke their parents. Their systems were overloaded from overscheduled days, their father's erratic absences on business trips, inconsistent meals, a weary, frustrated, often-angry mother, not to mention fears of monsters. Instead of winding down at bedtime, they wound up. Steven and Marcia assumed they weren't tired enough for bed. To grab some alone time, they let the kids watch television, which caused more revving than calming.

They didn't realize their children were beyond tired. It wasn't that they didn't want to sleep. They were dying to sleep, but their bodies had tension and energy that had to be released before calming down. Their parents had to see that the energy didn't build so high.

What Is the Behavior Signaling?

Remember, behavior is the expression of external stimuli combined with internal emotions. In this case, Nate's already anxious nature met with an unpredictable environment. The expression of this was similar to a wind-up toy. Bedtime frenzy was worse after an evening school event or soccer game, especially if he lost. He had tantrums over the slightest injustice and took it out on Shawna.

"And Shawna!" Marcia rolled her eyes. "She's getting her master's in bedtime manipulation. 'You promised another book' or 'I'm scared,' or 'I can't sleep.' And then the pitter-patter of those damn feet down the stairs or into our bedroom in the middle of the night is enough to drive me insane." The children's behavior tried to tell their parents they were too agitated to flip the switch into sleep mode, but their parents were too exhausted themselves to pick up the clues. The dimmer switch needed to start going down much earlier.

Is Acceptance Unconditional?

According to Mary Sheedy Kurcinka, author of *Sleepless in America,* three main triggers send children over the edge into problem sleep patterns: 1) how much tension is in their bodies from upset or excitement, 2) daily schedules or lack of routine, and 3) temperament—how much or how little each child is effected by external factors. With the Goreski children, all three areas were compromised.

After working with the principles, and understanding each of their children's temperaments, Marcia and Steven realized they were not responding to their children's needs. Marcia saw Shawna's demands for back rubs as manipulative rather than a physical adjustment to help her relax. And Nate's wind-up toy behavior was met with angry attempts at control. Soft, reassuring voices were what he needed to downshift. Nate feared monsters hiding behind the closet doors and in his toy basket. "How many times do you tell a kid there is no such thing before they believe you?" Marcia asked before she realized she needed to acknowledge his fear. Shawna was afraid to be alone. Her cries were pleading for companionship.

Sensitive temperaments can be an inconvenience for parents. Steven and Marcia didn't see the need to change their agendas for their children. They expected them to accommodate to their unstructured lives—after all what choice did they have? Unknowingly, they were not accepting who their children were.

Are Expectations Set for Success or Failure?

Marcia and Steven wanted adult alone time. But that was their agenda. Shawna and Nate needed to wind down and wanted to put off bedtime as long as possible—that was their agenda. Children don't understand their bodies' need for sleep—that's not their job. But they might not resist bedtime so much if their biological expectation is met. It helps to keep the perspective that co-sleeping is the norm for 90 percent of the world's population. A small child's physical expectation is to sleep with a warm body. Parents who choose not to co-sleep must make an effort to encourage children into comfortable, isolated sleep. Steven and Marcia needn't give up their agendas, but expecting their children to agreeably go off to bed to sleep alone is unrealistic.

When Steven heard Shawna's balking, he would argue, yell, and eventually give in to lying down with her, inevitably falling asleep and setting up bad habits and patterns of manipulation. Tense, angry reprimands only increase agitation making it nearly impossible for Shawna to acquiesce. A bedtime plan with a long, slow wind down sets a realistic expectation that children need help settling down for a night alone.

Is Connection Being Made?

Steven and Marcia made a list of their bedtime strategies and next to each wrote the words connect or disconnect. Understanding that disconnect strategies increased tension, they realized they had a ways to go to calm their children. Their connection strategies—cuddling, back rubs, and stories—occurred only occasionally.

When Marcia began recognizing the signals of Nate's revving up behavior around five o'clock, her new perspective allowed her to communicate empathically and accept his problem instead of expecting self-control. Learning connective communication, she tried nonblaming comments like, "Nate, your energy is buzzing like a bee," or "It looks like your insides are spinning around," or "You're moving into fourth gear. What do you need to bring yourself back to second?"

What Qualities Need Focus in Order to Grow?

Calm and peace were the words Steven used to describe what he thought they all needed. Now that they understood the children weren't getting wound up on purpose, he and Marcia focused on the triggers that set them off. Nate's stress increased with too many or inconsistent plans. Shawna argued and demanded more after an afternoon of television. Focusing on calm, they looked for ways to create it. Often a swing on the gym set helped Shawna, but Nate revved up on the swing, leading to aggression toward Shawna. Nate, they discovered, needed physical contact. Lots of hugging, even wrestling helped avert tantrums before dinner. As much as they thought soccer was a good energy release, Nate often sat out, and games and practices were at inconsistent times. Soccer could come back in his life when he was older and his system could handle more. Violin lessons were once a week—same day, same time. Practice at home could be made consistent too. It was clear which choice to make.

Then Steven and Marcia looked at themselves. They often argued in front of the kids. And morning squabbles were not infrequent, especially when sleep was "Shawna-disrupted." The only thing they agreed on these days was that both their children were unruly. They agreed to dissect their disagreements after the children were asleep. Steven decided he could get home earlier to spend more time with the kids if he worked from home at night when he was in town. Just keeping their focus dialed on "calm" adjusted their expectations. But it was easy to snap back into automatic reactions.

How Can the Problem Be Solved Without Punishment?

As a family, they wrote a bedtime contract (for more on contracts, see Chapter 7) starting with dinnertime. No TV after dinner made a huge difference. The kids argued this so to gain cooperation they agreed to try it for one month and marked a date on the calendar in red when they would reevaluate the decision. No one ever mentioned the reevaluation date. Dinnertime through bedtime meant mommy and daddy-time straight through. Cleanup waited. Steven usually got home by six and worked again after eight thirty. During nice weather, they were outdoors. Shawna could swing and Nate pushed sometimes. Often he had wrestling time with Dad. The physical contact helped Nate as long as Steven stopped it early enough. Family read replaced television, and then a marching game to the tune of "Nick, Knack, Paddy Whack" took them upstairs and became a nightly must.

Steven put Nate to bed for valuable talk time or boys' read, while Marcia stayed with Shawna and read their photo bedtime book. Marcia photographed all of them in their bedtime routine, from family read to baths to teeth brushing to snuggling in bed with Mom and Dad. Each picture had a caption dictated and then memorized by Shawna. A happy picture of the whole family ended the album. When Shawna begged for more time, Marcia gave her the choice of listening to water music, children's songs, or the book she had recorded in her voice to play on her tape recorder.

If Steven was away, Nate read and waited for his mommy-time after Marcia finished with Shawna. When Nate worried about invading monsters, they searched the room and the closet wielding Nerf bats. Then Marcia tucked his Nerf bat in beside him. Often they drew monster pictures and give them names and funny faces.

Then, Marcia sat in the hallway until they fell asleep. It took about a month before the hallway vigil could end. After that, hallway sitting was random if someone was having a hard night.

During the night, Shawna was given the choice of being walked back to her bed or sleeping on a doggie bed, purchased just for her, at the foot of her parents' bed. But the agreement was that if she kept them awake, she would lose her "doggie" privileges for that night. No miracle cures here, but the option of sleeping in her parents' room kept her asleep more often and out of their bed.

Are Strong Boundaries Keeping Good Balance?

No one had set any boundaries. Empty threats and manipulation created power imbalances, and no one took responsibility for their own problems. Steven and Marcia thought they were trapped in a bedtime nightmare. What they hadn't known was that simply giving more one-on-one attention from dinner on, sticking to a routine as often as possible, and taking everyone's needs and wishes into consideration were the basics of stopping the vicious cycles and climbing out of the trap. These were simple but hard patterns to change.

There is always a trial and error period in changing old habits. Wanting the change and being willing to commit are the first steps. Often one parent is ready and the other is not. Steven and Marcia had to take responsibility, put in the effort, and trust their children's desire for success. Once they held the perspective that the children were having problems settling down instead of fighting for control, their attitudes could shift. They had a bedtime contract they could point to when an argument arose. They could rewrite it as needs changed. It was Steven and Marcia's responsibility for all to hold to it.

The more it was expected that Nate and Shawna would argue and complain simply because they hated going to bed, not because they were obstinate and unruly, the calmer were their parents' reactions, and eventually the fewer were the arguments. Nate and Shawna needed a great deal of help before their bodies could relax and calm down. Evenings of predictable connection led to predictable bedtimes. Until this could be counted on, they kept exceptions to the routine at a minimum. They knew once patterns were set and the children were older, the routine could relax.

When everyone in the family can trust that their needs will be met and their voices heard, they don't have to yell so loudly. It's sometimes a long road to get there, especially when we were not brought up with this kind of trust, but the reward is great and family life is much easier. When we know that our children want to be successful and are not out to get us, and we are willing to support that success, they can be a joy to live with.

Final Notes

The Eight Principles of Confident Parenting:

1. My child wants to be successful (Success)
2. Behavior is my clue (Clues)
3. My child's greatest need is acceptance (Acceptance)
4. Expectations must be set for success (Expectations)
5. Connection strengthens relationship (Connection)
6. The behavior I focus on grows (Focus)
7. Problem solving, not punishment, teaches responsibility (Problem Solving)
8. Good boundaries mean good balance (Boundaries)

Your checklist of the principles:

1. How is your child's behavior intended for success?
   - What might your child's misbehavior help her avoid, be protecting her from?
   - Remember your child as a toddler. Was there enthusiasm and a desire to please? What got in his way?
   - Why would she not want to be successful? Remember that she is never happy being manipulative or out of control.
2. What is your child's behavior signaling?
   - Be a detective and look for any possible clues the behavior is giving. See the behavior as a red flag. What is your child trying to tell you?
   - Look for the roots beneath the behavior. Write down all you can think of whether or not they seem accurate. Ask

your partner, relatives, and close friends for roots they may see.

- What does her behavior tell you about her internal emotional state? What are the external conditions combining with those emotions?

3. Is your acceptance of your child unconditional?
   - Make a list of all your child's characteristics. Ask your partner, relatives, and close friends.
   - Determine what characteristics are due to inborn temperament and what are learned behaviors.
   - Ask yourself if you unconditionally accept all temperamental aspects of your child, or are you trying to change her to be who you want.

4. Are your expectations setting your child up for success or failure?
   - Ask yourself honestly what your standards of behavior are and what you expect your child to do or say. Is that realistic and appropriate given her temperament, individual learning style, and development?
   - Can your child meet your expectations successfully? If not, how can you adjust them to fit what he is capable of meeting successfully right now?
   - Name your expectations and ask yourself what messages they are sending to your child.

5. Are you making connection?
   - How do you typically react to your child's behavior? Do your reactions create a gap or encourage her to stay and work it out?
   - Does your child know that you will always accept his feelings and thoughts?
   - Remember to be a sounding board. Offer no advice, buts, or questions. Simply validate and empathize.

6. How can you focus on what you want to grow?

- Make sure your eyes and words reflect more positives than negatives. Be specific with appreciation. Don't praise generally.
- Name a quality you would like to see grow. Nurture it whenever you see it.
- What aspect of your child's demand or resistance can you point out positively, for example, "You really know what you want."

7. How can you solve the problem without punishment?

- Hold your child accountable. Wait until all emotions have cooled. State the problem, hers or yours, don't lay blame, and respectfully ask how it could have happened differently.
- Do ask questions to facilitate his thinking. Don't direct and tell him what to do.
- Set up consequences ahead of time as often as possible so your child knows what to expect. Offer a choice of the behavior or the consequence. Follow through. Write contracts when appropriate.

8. Are you keeping strong boundaries?

- Do you know the difference between your problems and your child's? Own your problems and ask for cooperation. Help but do not deny, rescue, or fix your child's problems.
- Are you taking responsibility for your problems and not expecting your child to solve them? Are you allowing your child to take responsibility for his problems and not developing his dependency on you to do the solving?
- The more you are able to detach and not take things personally, the better you are able to help, offer suggestions, and ask questions to facilitate your child's own problem solving.

Tips for Staying Calm:

- When emotions are heated, stop dangerous actions only. Do not react.
- Never try to teach a lesson or solve a problem in the heat of the moment.
- Walk away if you think you will yell, blame, or shame.
- Count to ten.
- Inhale and exhale deeply at least three times.
- Find a word or phrase to repeat to yourself that will hold you back from reacting even for a second.
- Remind yourself that your child is *having* a problem not *being* a problem.
- If your emotions are high, acknowledge that you are having a problem as well. Own it. Don't make your child responsible for your feelings or reactions.
- Don't take it personally. Do be a sounding board.
- Appeal to your child's sense of fairness and logic.
- Remember, this too will pass.

Suggestions

It's not easy to parent in ways that others may not agree with. Applying these eight principles will set you apart from the crowd. And the crowd may try to win you back. If these eight principles inspire you, if you want to raise your children by them, here are some suggestions to help you remain strong in your new knowledge and to encourage others to join you:

1. Write the principles down in your own words; words that will help you remember the key ideas of each one.
2. Create your own parenting group. Gather a group of friends and meet for an hour or two each week to discuss the principles and ways they can apply to your families. You can use

the main ideas listed at the end of each chapter to get things going. Choose some of the practices to do for homework.

3. Sign up for our discussion group to join with others from all over the world to learn how they are using the principles in their parenting. Visit my Web site, *www.bonnieharris.com*, and look under Resources to find the link.

4. Suggest *Confident Parents, Remarkable Kids* to your book group, church group, your children's teachers, principals, and school superintendents.

5. Give *Confident Parents, Remarkable Kids* to friends and family members to help them understand why you feel so strongly about parenting your children this way and to bring them on board.

6. Check to make sure your local library carries *Confident Parents, Remarkable Kids*. If it doesn't, request that they add it to their collection or consider donating a copy. Ask your family and friends in other towns and states to do the same.

7. Make sure that your local bookstores have the book on their shelves.

8. Write a book review for Amazon.com, Barnes and Noble, Borders, or comment on a parenting blog that you contribute to.

9. Read *When Your Kids Push Your Buttons and What You Can Do About It*. Often, our best intentions get derailed when our buttons get pushed, and what we want to put into practice feels out of our reach. We can have all the best parenting tools, but our buttons are our obstacles to putting them into practice. This book will help you understand what your buttons are, why your children push them, and how to take responsibility for them and defuse them so you can put these principles into practice.

About the Author

Bonnie Harris has been a parent educator and counselor for more than twenty years. She received her master's degree in Early Childhood Education from Bank Street College in New York City. She founded The Parent Guidance Center in Peterborough, New Hampshire in 1990, now The Family Center, and is the director of Connective Parenting. Bonnie is the author of *When Your Kids Push Your Buttons and What You Can Do About It* (Warner Books, 2003). She teaches her "Buttons" workshops and professional trainings and speaks internationally on a variety of parenting topics. She is the mother of two grown children and lives with her husband in Peterborough, New Hampshire.

www.connectiveparenting.com
bh@bonnieharris.com

Index

Acceptance, unconditional,
39–56
aggressive child and, 43–46
applied to bedtime, 212–13
applied to chores, 170–71
applied to homework, 196–97
applied to mealtime, 204–5
applied to morning rush,
162–63
applied to peer pressure,
188–89
applied to sibling rivalry,
178–79
as basic need of child, 28
checklist for, 219
child's wish for, 2–3, 7
"different" child and, 48–50
distractible child and, 53–54
fear and doubt and, 54–55
mirroring as, 46–48
strong-willed child and, 50–53
Accountability, logic and,
127–30
Agendas, connection and, 79
Aggressive children
acceptance and, 43–46
avoiding taking offense, 93–94
expectations and, 61
fear and anger and, 119
focusing on positive with,
100–101
Ally, being child's, 84–85
Anger, fear and, 119
Answer, not always having,
146–48
Appreciation, not expecting,
149–50
Attention, in connective
communication, 81

Authority, versus control, 116
Autocratic expectations,
11–13
Autocratic model of parenting,
22, 154

"Beat-Up Buddies," 88
Bedtime, principles applied to,
211–17
Behavior, as child's signal,
19–37. *See also* Focus, on good
behavior
applied to bedtime, 212
applied to chores, 170
applied to homework, 196
applied to mealtime, 204
applied to morning rush, 162
applied to peer pressure, 188
applied to sibling rivalry, 178
checklist for, 218
"childology" and, 32–34, 196
handling "dramatic," 31–32
hearing instead of reacting to,
28–32
as indicator of child's well-
being, 19–21
learning to interpret, 21–26,
37
misbehavior as attempt to be
successful, 5
obstacles and misbehavior,
26–28
physiological reasons for
misbehavior, 35–36
self-protection and, 35
understanding misbehavior,
26–28
Belonging, as basic need of child,
28